WALT WHITMAN

SELECTED POEMS

WALT WHITMAN

SELECTED POEMS

State Street Press

CONTENTS

INTRODUCTION

Walt Whitman was born in 1819 in West Hills, Huntington, Long Island, New York, and raised in Brooklyn. He seemed destined to live an uneventful and anonymous life. His father was an uneducated farmer and carpenter and Whitman himself left school at the age of thirteen to take a job as a newspaper office boy. Although he eventually worked his way up to become a reporter, book reviewer, and an editor, his newspaper writing, while competent, was neither original nor inspiring.

Then, in 1855, the virtually unknown Whitman, at the age of thirty-six, had a small volume of verse privately published. The book, *Leaves of Grass*, one of the most original and unconventional works in literature, marked the debut of the greatest poet America has yet produced. For sheer audacity the first edition of *Leaves of Grass* is unequaled in nineteenth-century literature. Whitman's poetry was a celebration of the common man, of American democracy, and of sexuality, conveyed through a revolutionary and rhapsodic free verse. Not even the English Romantics had broken so consciously and radically from poetic tradition.

Despite its originality, or perhaps because of it, *Leaves of Grass* would have sunk into obscurity had it not been for Ralph Waldo Emerson, the then dean of American letters and a major influence on Whitman. Upon receiving a copy he wrote to Whitman:

> I am not blind to the worth of the wonderful gift of *Leaves of Grass*. I find it the most extraordinary piece of wit and wisdom that America has yet contributed. I am very happy in reading it. I find incomparable things, said incomparably well, as they must be. . . . I greet you at the beginning of a great career. . . .

With this letter, which Whitman reprinted without Emerson's permission, he was able to promote his book.

America in the mid-nineteenth century was still a young and developing nation and one of Whitman's aims in his poetry was to break free of the cultural and political traditions of Europe and exalt the United States, its people, and democracy, in a new and uniquely American poetry. He believed this country had a special place in the history of the world as its first true, working democracy. His best poetry radiates an almost boundless faith and promise in the capability of the United States and its citizens.

During the Civil War, Whitman's faith in America was put to a severe test. His brother George, a Union soldier, was wounded in battle and in 1862 Whitman went to visit him at the camp near Washington, D.C. where he was recovering. He remained in Washington for the duration of the war comforting and helping to nurse the wounded in hospitals there. It was a traumatic experience for him as he faced first-hand the suffering and deaths of thousands of American men. It inspired him to write the poems which would later become the *Drum-Taps* and the *Sequel to Drum-Taps* sections of *Leaves of Grass*, which includes the justly famous "When Lilacs Last in the Dooryard Bloom'd," his moving elegy for the assassinated president, Abraham Lincoln. Many critics believe that Whitman's Civil War experiences destroyed him as a poet, because in the post-war years he rarely wrote with his earlier inspiration and produced few great poems.

After the war, Whitman's reputation continued to grow, especially in England. Most people, however, considered his poetry scandalous and it even cost him his job as a clerk in the Department of Interior because James Harlan, then Secretary, disapproved of it.

In 1873, after suffering a paralytic stroke, Whitman retired to Camden, New Jersey. There he became a true American sage, "the good gray poet"—in the words of the title of one of many biographies written during his lifetime—surrounded by disciples and supporters. When he died in 1892, he was a revered and internationally famous poet.

The years since Whitman's death have seen the estimation of his poetry grow and his stature as America's greatest poet secured, for no other poet in our history has ever created as grand and inspiring a vision of America and its seemingly infinite promise.

Walt Whitman wrote only one book of poetry—*Leaves of Grass*. From its first publication until his death, it went through numerous editions in which he added poems, revised many, and rearranged their order. This collection presents chronologically Walt Whitman's most famous and greatest work. All the selections here include his final revisions except for the first seven poems which are presented as they appeared in the first edition of *Leaves of Grass*, since the original versions are considered more spontaneous and innovative than Whitman's later changes. He himself said, "I do not suppose that I shall ever again have the *afflatus* [inspiration] I had in writing the first *Leaves of Grass*." Also included are excerpts from Whitman's original preface to the 1855 edition of *Leaves of Grass* in which he explains his theory for a new American poetry.

CHRISTOPHER MOORE

New York
1992

EXCERPTS FROM
PREFACE TO LEAVES OF GRASS
1855

The Americans of all nations at any time upon the earth have probably the fullest poetical nature. The United States themselves are essentially the greatest poem. In the history of the earth hitherto, the largest and most stirring appear tame and orderly to their ampler largeness and stir. Here at last is something in the doings of man that corresponds with the broadcast doings of the day and night. Here is not merely a nation but a teeming nation of nations. Here is action untied from strings necessarily blind to particulars and details magnificently moving in vast masses. Here is the hospitality which forever indicates heroes. . . . Here are the roughs and beards and space and ruggedness and nonchalance that the soul loves. Here the performance disdaining the trivial unapproached in the tremendous audacity of its crowds and groupings and the push of its perspective spreads with crampless and flowing breadth and showers its prolific and splendid extravagance. One sees it must indeed own the riches of the summer and winter, and need never be bankrupt while corn grows from the ground, or the orchards drop apples, or the bays contain fish, or men beget children upon women.

✿　✿　✿

The land and sea, the animals, fishes and birds, the sky of heaven and the orbs, the forests, mountains and rivers, are not small themes . . . but folks expect of the poet to indicate more than the beauty and dignity which always attach to dumb real objects . . . they expect him to indicate the path between reality and their souls. Men and women perceive the beauty well enough . . . probably as well as he. The passionate tenacity of hunters, woodmen, early risers, cultivators of gardens and orchards and fields, the love of healthy women for the manly form, seafaring persons, drivers of horses, the passion for light and the open air, all is an old varied sign of the unfailing perception of beauty, and of a residence of the poetic in outdoor people. They can never be assisted by poets to perceive . . . some may but they never can. The poetic quality is not marshalled in rhyme or uniformity, or abstract addresses to things, nor in melancholy complaints or good precepts, but is the life of these and much else, and is in the soul. The profit of rhyme is that it drops seeds of a sweeter and more luxuriant rhyme, and of uniformity that it conveys itself into its own roots in the ground out of sight. The rhyme and uniformity of perfect poems show the free growth of metrical laws and bud from them as unerringly and loosely as lilacs or roses on a bush, and take shapes as compact as the shapes of chestnuts and oranges and melons and pears, and shed the perfume impalpable to form. The fluency and ornaments of the finest poems or music or orations or recitations, are not independent but dependent. All beauty comes from beautiful blood and a beautiful brain. If the greatnesses are in conjunction in a man or woman, it is enough . . . the fact will prevail through the universe . . . but the gaggery and gilt of a million years will not prevail. Who troubles himself about his ornaments or fluency is lost. This is what you shall do: Love the earth and sun and the animals, despise riches, give alms to every one that asks, stand up for the stupid and crazy, devote your income and labor to others, hate tyrants, argue not concerning God, have patience and indulgence toward the people, take off your hat to nothing known or unknown, or to any man or number of men, go freely with powerful uneducated persons, and with the young, and with the mothers of families, read these leaves in the open air every season of every year of your life, re-examine all you have been told at school or church or in any book, dismiss whatever insults your own soul, and your very flesh shall be a great poem and have the richest fluency, not only in its words, but in the silent lines of its lips and face, and between the lashes of your eyes, and in every motion and joint of your body. The poet shall not spend his time in unneeded work. He shall know that the ground is always already ploughed and manured . . . others may not know it but he shall. He shall go directly to the creation. His trust shall master the trust of everything he touches . . . and shall master all attachment.

✿   ✿   ✿

The American bards shall be marked for generosity and affection, and for encouraging competitors . . . They shall be kosmos . . . without monopoly or secrecy . . . glad to pass any thing to any one . . . hungry for equals night and day. They shall not be careful of riches and privilege . . . they shall be riches and privilege . . . they shall perceive who the most affluent man is. The most affluent man is he that confronts all the shows he sees by equivalents out of the stronger wealth of himself. The American bard shall delineate no class of persons nor one or two out of the strata of interests nor love most nor truth most, nor the soul most, nor the body most . . . and not be for the eastern states more than the western, or the northern states more than the southern.

❖   ❖   ❖

There will soon be no more priests. Their work is done. They may wait awhile . . . perhaps a generation or two . . . dropping off by degrees. A superior breed shall take their place . . . the gangs of kosmos and prophets en masse shall take their place. A new order shall arise, and they shall be the priests of man, and every man shall be his own priest. The churches built under their umbrage shall be the churches of men and women. Through the divinity of themselves shall the kosmos and the new breed of poets be interpreters of men and women and of all events and things. They shall find their inspiration in real objects today, symptoms of the past and future. . . . They shall not deign to defend immortality or God, or the perfection of things, or liberty, or the exquisite beauty and reality of the soul. They shall arise in America and be responded to from the remainder of the earth.

The English language befriends the grand American expression . . . it is brawny enough, and limber and full enough. On the tough stock of a race who through all change of circumstances was never without the idea of political liberty, which is the animus of all liberty, it has attracted the terms of daintier and gayer and subtler and more elegant tongues. It is the powerful language of resistance . . . it is the dialect of common sense. It is the speech of the proud and melancholy races, and of all who aspire. It is the chosen tongue to express growth, faith, self-esteem, freedom, justice, equality, friendliness, amplitude, prudence, decision, and courage. It is the medium that shall well nigh express the inexpressible.

[EUROPE: THE 72D AND 73D YEARS
OF THESE STATES]

Suddenly out of its stale and drowsy lair, the lair of slaves,
Like lightning Europe le'pt forth . . . . half startled at itself,
Its feet upon the ashes and the rags . . . . Its hands tight
    to the throats of kings.

O hope and faith! O aching close of lives! O many
    a sickened heart!
Turn back unto this day, and make yourselves afresh.

And you, paid to defile the People . . . . you liars mark:
Not for numberless agonies, murders, lusts,
For court thieving in its manifold mean forms,
Worming from his simplicity the poor man's wages;
For many a promise sworn by royal lips, and broken, and
    laughed at in the breaking,
Then in their power not for all these did the blows strike of
    personal revenge . . or the heads of the nobles fall;
The People scorned the ferocity of kings.

But the sweetness of mercy brewed bitter destruction,
    and the frightened rulers come back:
Each comes in state with his train . . . . hangman, priest and
    tax-gatherer . . . . soldier, lawyer, jailer and sycophant.

Yet behind all, lo, a Shape,
Vague as the night, draped interminably, head front
    and form in scarlet folds,
Whose face and eyes none may see,
Out of its robes only this . . . . the red robes, lifted
    by the arm,
One finger pointed high over the top, like the head of
    a snake appears.

Meanwhile corpses lie in new-made graves . . . . bloody
corpses of young men:
The rope of the gibbet hangs heavily . . . . the bullets of
princes are flying . . . . the creatures of power laugh aloud,
And all these things bear fruits . . . . and they are good.

Those corpses of young men,
Those martyrs that hang from the gibbets . . . those hearts
pierced by the gray lead,
Cold and motionless as they seem . . live elsewhere with
unslaughter'd vitality.

They live in other young men, O kings,
They live in brothers, again ready to defy you:
They were purified by death . . . . they were taught and exalted.

Not a grave of the murdered for freedom but grows
seed for freedom . . . . in its turn to bear seed,
Which the winds carry afar and re-sow, and the rains and
the snows nourish.

Not a disembodied spirit can the weapons of tyrants let loose,
But it stalks invisibly over the earth . . whispering
counseling cautioning.

Liberty let others despair of you . . . . I never despair of you.

Is the house shut? Is the master away?
Nevertheless be ready . . . . be not weary of watching.
He will soon return . . . . his messengers come anon.

[1850]

[SONG OF MYSELF]

[1]

I celebrate myself,
And what I assume you shall assume,
For every atom belonging to me as good belongs to you.

I loafe and invite my soul,
I lean and loafe at my ease .... observing a spear of
   summer grass.

[2]

Houses and rooms are full of perfumes .... the shelves are
   crowded with perfumes,
I breathe the fragrance myself, and know it and like it,
The distillation would intoxicate me also, but I shall
   not let it.

The atmosphere is not a perfume .... it has no taste of the
   distillation .... it is odorless,
It is for my mouth forever .... I am in love with it,
I will go to the bank by the wood and become undisguised
   and naked,
I am mad for it to be in contact with me.

The smoke of my own breath,
Echoes, ripples, and buzzed whispers .... loveroot,
   silkthread, crotch and vine,
My respiration and inspiration .... the beating of my heart
   .... the passing of blood and air through my lungs,
The sniff of green leaves and dry leaves, and of the shore
   and darkcolored sea-rocks, and of hay in the barn,
The sound of the belched words of my voice .... words
   loosed to the eddies of the wind,

A few light kisses .... a few embraces .... a reaching
    around of arms,
The play of shine and shade on the trees as the supple
    boughs wag.
The delight alone or in the rush of the streets, or along the
    fields and hillsides,
The feeling of health .... the full-noon trill .... the song
    of me rising from bed and meeting the sun.

Have you reckoned a thousand acres much? Have you
    reckoned the earth much?
Have you practiced so long to learn to read?
Have you felt so proud to get at the meaning of poems?

Stop this day and night with me and you shall possess the
    origin of all poems,
You shall possess the good of the earth and sun ....
    there are millions of suns left,
You shall no longer take things at second or third hand ....
    nor look through the eyes of the dead .... nor feed
    on the spectres in books,
You shall not look through my eyes either, nor take things
    from me,
You shall listen to all sides and filter them from yourself.

    [3]
I have heard what the talkers were talking .... the
    talk of the beginning and the end,
But I do not talk of the beginning or the end.

There was never any more inception than there is now,
Nor any more youth or age than there is now;
And will never be any more perfection than there is now,
Nor any more heaven or hell than there is now.

Urge and urge and urge,
Always the procreant urge of the world.

Out of the dimness opposite equals advance . . . . Always
    substance and increase,
Always a knit of identity . . . . always distinction . . . .
    always a breed of life.

To elaborate is no avail . . . . Learned and unlearned feel
    that it is so.

Sure as the most certain sure . . . . plumb in the uprights,
    well entretied, braced in the beams,
Stout as a horse, affectionate, haughty, electrical,
I and this mystery here we stand.

Clear and sweet is my soul . . . . and clear and sweet
    is all that is not my soul.

Lack one lacks both . . . . and the unseen is proved
    by the seen,
Till that becomes unseen and receives proof in its turn.

Showing the best and dividing it from the worst,
    age vexes age,
Knowing the perfect fitness and equanimity of things, while
    they discuss I am silent, and go bathe and admire myself.

Welcome is every organ and attribute of me, and of any
    man hearty and clean,
Not an inch nor a particle of an inch is vile, and none
    shall be less familiar than the rest.

I am satisfied . . . . I see, dance, laugh, sing;
As God comes a loving bedfellow and sleeps at my side all
    night and close on the peep of the day,
And leaves for me baskets covered with white towels
    bulging the house with their plenty.

Shall I postpone my acceptation and realization and
    scream at my eyes,
That they turn from gazing after and down the road,
And forthwith cipher and show me to a cent,
Exactly the contents of one, and exactly the contents of
    two, and which is ahead?

   [4]

Trippers and askers surround me,
People I meet . . . . the effect upon me of my early life . . . .
    of the ward and city I live in . . . . of the nation,
The latest news . . . . discoveries, inventions, societies . . . .
    authors old and new,
My dinner, dress, associates, looks, business, compliments,
    dues,
The real or fancied indifference of some man or woman
    I love,
The sickness of one of my folks—or of myself . . . . or
    ill-doing . . . . or loss or lack of money . . . . or
    depressions or exaltations,
They come to me days and nights and go from me again,
But they are not the Me myself.

Apart from the pulling and hauling stands what I am,
Stands amused, complacent, compassionating, idle, unitary,
Looks down, is erect, bends an arm on an impalpable
    certain rest,
Looks with its sidecurved head curious what will come next,
Both in and out of the game, and watching and wondering
    at it.

Backward I see in my own days where I sweated through fog
    with linguists and contenders,
I have no mockings or arguments . . . . I witness and wait.

[5]
I believe in you my soul ... . the other I am must not abase
    itself to you,
And you must not be abased to the other.

Loafe with me on the grass ... . loose the stop from your
    throat,
Not words, not music or rhyme I want ... . not custom or
    lecture, not even the best,
Only the lull I like, the hum of your valved voice.
I mind how we lay in June, such a transparent summer
    morning;
You settled your head athwart my hips and gently turned
    over upon me,
And parted the shirt from my bosom-bone, and plunged
    your tongue to my barestript heart,
And reached till you felt my beard, and reached till you held
    my feet.

Swiftly arose and spread around me the peace and joy and
    knowledge that pass all the art and argument of
    the earth;
And I know that the hand of God is the elderhand of my own,
And I know that the spirit of God is the eldest brother
    of my own,
And that all the men ever born are also my brothers ... .
    and the women my sisters and lovers,
And that a kelson of the creation is love;
And limitless are leaves stiff or drooping in the fields,
And brown ants in the little wells beneath them,
And mossy scabs of the wormfence, and heaped stones,
    and elder and mullen and pokeweed.

[6]

A child said, What is the grass? fetching it to me with full
    hands;
How could I answer the child? . . . . I do not know what it is
    any more than he.

I guess it must be the flag of my disposition, out of hopeful
    green stuff woven.

Or I guess it is the handkerchief of the Lord,
A scented gift and remembrancer designedly dropped,
Bearing the owner's name someway in the corners, that we
    may see and remark, and say Whose?

Or I guess the grass is itself a child . . . . the produced babe
    of the vegetation.
Or I guess it is a uniform hieroglyphic,
And it means, Sprouting alike in broad zones and narrow
    zones,
Growing among black folks as among white,
Kanuck, Tuckahoe, Congressman, Cuff, I give them the
    same, I receive them the same.
And now it seems to me the beautiful uncut hair of graves.

Tenderly will I use you curling grass,
It may be you transpire from the breasts of young men,
It may be if I had known them I would have loved them;
It may be you are from old people and from women, and
        from offspring taken soon out of their mothers' laps,
And here you are the mothers' laps.

This grass is very dark to be from the white heads of
    old mothers,
Darker than the colorless beards of old men,
Dark to come from under the faint red roofs of mouths.

O I perceive after all so many uttering tongues!
And I perceive they do not come from the roofs of mouths
    for nothing.

I wish I could translate the hints about the dead young men
    and women,
And the hints about old men and mothers, and the offspring
    taken soon out of their laps.

What do you think has become of the young and old men?
And what do you think has become of the women and
    children?

They are alive and well somewhere;
The smallest sprout shows there is really no death,
And if ever there was it led forward life, and does not wait
    at the end to arrest it,
And ceased the moment life appeared.

All goes onward and outward . . . . and nothing collapses,
And to die is different from what any one supposed, and
    luckier.

   [7]
Has any one supposed it lucky to be born?
I hasten to inform him or her it is just as lucky to die,
    and I know it.

I pass death with the dying, and birth with the new-washed
    babe . . . . and am not contained between my hat
    and boots,
And peruse manifold objects, no two alike, and every one
    good,
The earth good, and the stars good, and their adjuncts
    all good.

I am not an earth nor an adjunct of an earth,
I am the mate and companion of people, all just as immortal
and fathomless as myself;
They do not know how immortal, but I know.

Every kind for itself and its own . . . . for me mine male
and female,
For me all that have been boys and that love women,
For me the man that is proud and feels how it stings to be
slighted,
For me the sweetheart and the old maid . . . . for me mothers
and the mothers of mothers,
For me lips that have smiled, eyes that have shed tears,
For me children and the begetters of children.

Who need be afraid of the merge?
Undrape . . . . you are not guilty to me, nor stale nor
discarded,
I see through the broadcloth and gingham whether or no,
And am around, tenacious, acquisitive, tireless . . . . and can
never be shaken away.

[8]
The little one sleeps in its cradle,
I lift the gauze and look a long time, and silently brush away
flies with my hand.

The youngster and the redfaced girl turn aside up the
bushy hill,
I peeringly view them from the top.

The suicide sprawls on the bloody floor of the bedroom.
It is so . . . . I witnessed the corpse . . . . there the pistol had
fallen.

The blab of the pave . . . . the tires of carts and sluff of
bootsoles and talk of the promenaders,

The heavy omnibus, the driver with his interrogating thumb,
the clank of the shod horses on the granite floor,
The carnival of sleighs, the clinking and shouted jokes and
pelts of snowballs;
The hurrahs for popular favorites . . . . the fury of roused
mobs,
The flap of the curtained litter—the sick man inside,
borne to the hospital,
The meeting of enemies, the sudden oath, the blows and fall,
The excited crowd—the policeman with his star quickly
working his passage to the centre of the crowd;
The impassive stones that receive and return so many echoes,
The souls moving along . . . . are they invisible while the
least atom of the stones is visible?
What groans of overfed or half-starved who fall on the flags
sunstruck or in fits,
What exclamations of women taken suddenly, who hurry
home and give birth to babes,
What living and buried speech is always vibrating here . . . .
what howls restrained by decorum,
Arrests of criminals, slights, adulterous offers made,
acceptances, rejections with convex lips,
I mind them or the resonance of them . . . . I come again
and again.

[9]
The big doors of the country-barn stand open and ready,
The dried grass of the harvest-time loads the slow-drawn
wagon.
The clear light plays on the brown gray and green
intertinged,
The armfuls are packed to the sagging mow:
I am there . . . . I help . . . . I came stretched atop of the load,
I felt its soft jolts . . . . one leg reclined on the other,
I jump from the crossbeams, and seize the clover and
timothy.
And roll head over heels, and tangle my hair full of wisps.

[10]
Alone far in the wilds and mountains I hunt,
Wandering amazed at my own lightness and glee,
In the late afternoon choosing a safe spot to pass the night,
Kindling a fire and broiling the freshkilled game,
Soundly falling asleep on the gathered leaves, my dog and
    gun by my side.

The Yankee clipper is under her three skysails . . . . she cuts
    the sparkle and scud,
My eyes settle the land . . . . I bend at her prow or shout
    joyously from the deck.

The boatmen and clamdiggers arose early and stopped for me,
I tucked my trowser-ends in my boots and went and had a
    good time,
You should have been with us that day round the
    chowder-kettle.

I saw the marriage of the trapper in the open air in the
    far-west . . . . the bride was a red girl,
Her father and his friends sat near by crosslegged and
    dumbly smoking . . . . they had moccasins to their feet
    and large thick blankets hanging from their shoulders;
On a bank lounged the trapper . . . . he was dressed mostly
    in skins . . . . his luxuriant beard and curls protected
    his neck,
One hand rested on his rifle . . . . the other hand held firmly
    the wrist of the red girl,
She had long eyelashes . . . . her head was bare . . . . her coarse
    straight locks descended upon her voluptuous limbs
    and reached to her feet.

The runaway slave came to my house and stopped outside,
I heard his motions crackling the twigs of the woodpile,

Through the swung half-door of the kitchen I saw him
    limpsey and weak,
And went where he sat on a log, and led him in and assured
    him.
And brought water and filled a tub for his sweated body and
    bruised feet,
And gave him a room that entered from my own, and gave him
    some coarse clean clothes,
And remember perfectly well his revolving eyes and his
    awkwardness,
And remember putting plasters on the galls of his neck and ankles;
He staid with me a week before he was recuperated and
    passed north,
I had him sit next me at table .... my firelock leaned in the
    corner.

   [11]
Twenty-eight young men bathe by the shore,
Twenty-eight young men, and all so friendly,
Twenty-eight years of womanly life, and all so lonesome.

She owns the fine house by the rise of the bank.
She hides handsome and richly drest aft the blinds of the
    window.

Which of the young men does she like the best?
Ah the homeliest of them is beautiful to her.

Where are you off to, lady? for I see you,
You splash in the water there, yet stay stock still in your room.

Dancing and laughing along the beach came the twenty-ninth
    bather,
The rest did not see her, but she saw them and loved them.

The beards of the young men glistened with wet, it ran from
     their long hair,
Little streams passed all over their bodies.

An unseen hand also passed over their bodies,
It descended tremblingly from their temples ribs.

The young men float on their backs, their white bellies swell
     to the sun . . . . they do not ask who seizes fast to them,
They do not know who puffs and declines with pendant
     and bending arch,
They do not think whom they souse with spray.

[12]
The butcher-boy puts off his killing clothes, or sharpens his
     knife at the stall in the market,
I loiter enjoying his repartee and his shuffle and breakdown.

Blacksmiths with grimed and hairy chests environ the anvil,
Each has his main-sledge . . . . they are all out . . . . there is
     a great heat in the fire.

From the cinder-strewed threshold I follow their movements,
The lithe sheer of their waists plays even with their
     massive arms,
Overhand the hammers roll—overhand so slow—overhand
     so sure,
They do not hasten, each man hits in his place.

[13]
The negro holds firmly the reins of his four horses . . . . the
     block swags underneath on its tied-over chain,
The negro that drives the huge dray of the stoneyard . . . .
     steady and tall he stands poised on one leg on
     the stringpiece,

His blue shirt exposes his ample neck and breast and
     loosens over his hipband,
His glance is calm and commanding . . . . he tosses the
     slouch of his hat away from his forehead,
The sun falls on his crispy hair and moustache . . . . falls on
     The black of his polish'd and perfect limbs.

I behold the picturesque giant and love him . . . . and I do
     not stop there,
I go with the team also.

In me the caresser of life wherever moving . . . . backward
     as well as forward slueing,
To niches aside and junior bending.

Oxen that rattle the yoke or halt in the shade, what is
     that you express in your eyes?
It seems to me more than all the print I have read in my life.

My tread scares the wood-drake and wood-duck on my
     distant and daylong ramble,
They rise together, they slowly circle around.
    . . . . I believe in those winged purposes,
And acknowledge the red yellow and white playing
     within me,
And consider the green and violet and the tufted crown
     intentional;
And do not call the tortoise unworthy because she is
     not something else,
And the mocking bird in the swamp never studied the
     gamut, yet trills pretty well to me,
And the look of the bay mare shames silliness out of me.

[14]
The wild gander leads his flock through the cool night,
Ya-honk! he says, and sounds it down to me like an
     invitation;

The pert may suppose it meaningless, but I listen closer,
I find its purpose and place up there toward the
    November sky.

The sharphoofed moose of the north, the cat on the
    housesill, the chickadee, the prairie-dog,
The litter of the grunting sow as they tug at her teats,
The brood of the turkeyhen, and she with her halfspread
    wings,
I see in them and myself the same old law.

The press of my foot to the earth springs a hundred
    affections,
They scorn the best I can do to relate them.

I am enamoured of growing outdoors,
Of men that live among cattle or taste of the ocean or woods,
Of the builders and steerers of ships, of the wielders of
    axes and mauls, of the drivers of horses,
I can eat and sleep with them week in and week out.

What is commonest and cheapest and nearest and
    easiest is Me,
Me going in for my chances, spending for vast returns,
Adorning myself to bestow myself on the first that will
    take me,
Not asking the sky to come down to my goodwill,
Scattering it freely forever.

    [15]
The pure contralto sings in the organloft,
The carpenter dresses his plank . . . . the tongue of his
    foreplane whistles its wild ascending lisp,
The married and unmarried children ride home to their
    thanksgiving dinner,
The pilot seizes the king-pin, he heaves down with a
    strong arm,

The mate stands braced in the whaleboat, lance and
    harpoon are ready,
The duck-shooter walks by silent and cautious stretches,
The deacons are ordained with crossed hands at the altar,
The spinning-girl retreats and advances to the hum of the
    big wheel,
The farmer stops by the bars of a Sunday and looks at
    the oats and rye,
The lunatic is carried at last to the asylum a confirmed case,
He will never sleep any more as he did in the cot in his
    mother's bedroom;
The jour printer with gray head and gaunt jaws works
    at his case,
He turns his quid of tobacco, his eyes get blurred with
    the manuscript;
The malformed limbs are tied to the anatomist's table,
What is removed drops horribly in a pail;
The quadroon girl is sold at the stand .... the drunkard nods
    by the barroom stove,
The machinist rolls up his sleeves .... the policeman
    travels his beat .... the gatekeeper marks who pass,
The young fellow drives the express-wagon .... I love
    him though I do not know him;
The half-breed straps on his light boots to compete
    in the race,
The western turkey-shooting draws old and young ....
    some lean on their rifles, some sit on logs,
Out from the crowd steps the marksman and takes his
    position and levels his piece;
The groups of newly-come immigrants cover the wharf
    or levee,
The woollypates hoe in the sugarfield, the overseer
    views them from his saddle;
The bugle calls in the ballroom, the gentlemen run for their
    partners, the dancers bow to each other;
The youth lies awake in the cedar-roofed garret and
    harks to the musical rain,

The Wolverine sets traps on the creek that helps fill
    the Huron,
The reformer ascends the platform, he spouts with his
    mouth and nose,
The company returns from its excursion, the darkey
    brings up the rear and bears the well-riddled target,
The squaw wrapt in her yellow-hemmed cloth is
    offering moccasins and beadbags for sale,
The connoisseur peers along the exhibition-gallery with
    halfshut eyes bent sideways,
The deckhands make fast the steamboat, the plank is
    thrown for the shoregoing passengers,
The young sister holds out the skein, the elder sister winds it
    off in a ball and stops now and then for the knots,
The one-year wife is recovering and happy, a week
    ago she bore her first child,
The cleanhaired Yankee girl works with her sewing-machine
    or in the factory or mill,
The nine months' gone is in the parturition chamber, her
    faintness and pains are advancing;
The pavingman leans on his twohanded rammer—
    the reporter's lead flies swiftly over the notebook—
    the signpainter is lettering with red and gold,
The canal-boy trots on the towpath—the bookkeeper
    counts at his desk—the shoemaker waves his thread,
The conductor beats time for the band and all the
    performers follow him,
The child is baptised—the convert is making the first
    professions,
The regatta is spread on the bay .... how the white
    sails sparkle!
The drover watches his drove, he sings out to them
    that would stray,
The pedlar sweats with his pack on his back—the
    purchaser higgles about the odd cent,

The camera and plate are prepared, the lady must sit
 for her daguerreotype,
The bride unrumples her white dress, the minutehand
 of the clock moves slowly,
The opium eater reclines with rigid head and
 just-opened lips,
The prostitute draggles her shawl, her bonnet bobs
 on her tipsy and pimpled neck,
The crowd laugh at her blackguard oaths, the men jeer
 and wink to each other,
(Miserable! I do not laugh at your oaths nor jeer you,)
The President holds a cabinet council, he is surrounded
 by the great secretaries,
On the piazza walk five friendly matrons with twined arms;
The crew of the fish-smack pack repeated layers of
 halibut in the hold,
The Missourian crosses the plains toting his wares and
 his cattle,
The fare-collector goes through the train—he gives
 notice by the jingling of loose change,
The floormen are laying the floor—the tinners are tinning
 the roof—the masons are calling for mortar,
In single file each shouldering his hod pass onward
 the laborers;
Seasons pursuing each other the indescribable crowd
 is gathered . . . . it is the Fourth of July . . . . what salutes
 of cannon and small arms!
Seasons pursuing each other the plougher ploughs and
 the mower mows and the winter grain falls in the ground;
Off on the lakes the pikefisher watches and waits by the
 hole in the frozen surface,
The stumps stand thick round the clearing, the squatter
 strikes deep with his axe,
The flatboatmen make fast toward dusk near the
 cottonwood or pekantrees,

The coon-seekers go now through the regions of the
      Red river, or through those drained by the Tennessee,
      or through those of the Arkansas,
The torches shine in the dark that hangs on the
      Chattahoochee or Altamahaw;
Patriarchs sit at supper with sons and grandsons and
      great grandsons around them,
In walls of adobie, in canvas tents, rest hunters and
      trappers after their day's sport.
The city sleeps and the country sleeps,
The living sleep for their time .... the dead sleep for
      their time,
The old husband sleeps by his wife and the young
      husband sleeps by his wife;
And these one and all tend inward to me, and I tend
      outward to them,
And such as it is to be of these more or less I am.

[16]
I am of old and young, of the foolish as much as the wise,
Regardless of others, ever regardful of others,
Maternal as well as paternal, a child as well as a man,
Stuffed with the stuff that is coarse, and stuffed with
      the stuff that is fine,
One of the great nations, the nation of many nations—
      the smallest the same and the largest the same,
A southerner soon as a northerner, a planter nonchalant
      and hospitable,
A Yankee bound my own way .... ready for trade ....
      my joints the limberest joints on earth and the
      sternest joints on earth,
A Kentuckian walking the vale of the Elkhorn in my
      deerskin leggings,
A boatman over the lakes or bays or along coasts ....
      a Hoosier, a Badger, a Buckeye,
A Louisianian or Georgian, a poke-easy from sandhills
      and pines,

At home on Canadian snowshoes or up in the bush,
    or with fishermen off Newfoundland,
At home in the fleet of iceboats, sailing with the rest
    and tacking,
At home on the hills of Vermont or in the woods of
    Maine or the Texan ranch,
Comrade of Californians .... comrade of free
    northwesterners, loving their big proportions,
Comrade of raftsmen and coalmen—comrade of all who
    shake hands and welcome to drink and meat;
A learner with the simplest, a teacher of the thoughtfulest,
A novice beginning experient of myriads of seasons,
Of every hue and trade and rank, of every caste
    and religion,
Not merely of the New World but of Africa Europe or
    Asia .... a wandering savage,
A farmer, mechanic, or artist .... a gentleman, sailor,
    lover or quaker,
A prisoner, fancy-man, rowdy, lawyer, physician or priest.

I resist anything better than my own diversity,
And breathe the air and leave plenty after me,
And am not stuck up, and am in my place.

The moth and the fisheggs are in their place,
The suns I see and the suns I cannot see are in their place.
The palpable is in its place and the impalpable is in its place.

[17]
These are the thoughts of all men in all ages and lands,
    they are not original with me,
If they are not yours as much as mine they are nothing
    or next to nothing,
If they do not enclose everything they are next to nothing,
If they are not the riddle and the untying of the riddle
    they are nothing,
If they are not just as close as they are distant they
    are nothing.

This is the grass that grows wherever the land is and the
    water is,
This is the common air that bathes the globe.

This is the breath of laws and songs and behaviour,
This is the tasteless water of souls . . . . this is the true
    sustenance,
It is for the illiterate . . . . it is for the judges of the
    supreme court . . . . it is for the federal capitol and
    the state capitols,
It is for the admirable communes of literary men and
    composers and singers and lecturers and engineers
    and savans,
It is for the endless races of working people and
    farmers and seamen.

[18]
This is the trill of a thousand clear cornets and scream
    of the octave flute and strike of triangles.

I play not a march for victors only . . . . I play great
    marches for conquered and slain persons.

Have you heard that it was good to gain the day?
I also say it is good to fall . . . . battles are lost in the same
    spirit in which they are won.

I sound triumphal drums for the dead . . . . I fling through
    my embouchures the loudest and gayest music to them,
Vivas to those who have failed, and to those whose
    war-vessels sank in the sea, and those themselves
    who sank in the sea,
And to all generals that lost engagements, and all
    overcome heroes, and the numberless unknown heroes
    equal to the greatest heroes known.

[19]

This is the meal pleasantly set . . . . this is the meat and
    drink for natural hunger,
It is for the wicked just the same as the righteous . . . .
    I make appointments with all,
I will not have a single person slighted or left away,
The keptwoman and sponger and thief are hereby invited
    . . . . the heavy-lipped slave is invited . . . . the
    venerealee is invited,
There shall be no difference between them and the rest.

This is the press of a bashful hand . . . . this is the float
    and odor of hair,
This is the touch of my lips to yours . . . . this is the
    murmur of yearning,
This is the far-off depth and height reflecting my own face,
This is the thoughtful merge of myself and the outlet again.

Do you guess I have some intricate purpose?
Well I have . . . . for the April rain has, and the mica
    on the side of a rock has.

Do you take it I would astonish?
Does the daylight astonish? or the early redstart twittering
    through the woods?
Do I astonish more than they?

This hour I tell things in confidence,
I might not tell everybody but I will tell you.

[20]

Who goes there! hankering, gross, mystical, nude?
How is it I extract strength from the beef I eat?

What is a man anyhow? What am I? and what are you?
All I mark as my own you shall offset it with your own,
Else it were time lost listening to me.

I do not snivel that snivel the world over,
That months are vacuums and the ground but wallow
      and filth,
That life is a suck and a sell, and nothing remains at the
      end but threadbare crape and tears.

Whimpering and truckling fold with powders for
      invalids . . . . conformity goes to the fourth-removed,
I cock my hat as I please indoors or out.

Shall I pray? Shall I venerate and be ceremonious?
I have pried through the strata and analyzed to a hair,
And counselled with doctors and calculated close
      and found no sweeter fat than sticks to my own bones.

In all people I see myself, none more and not one a
      barleycorn less,
And the good or bad I say of myself I say of them.

And I know I am solid and sound,
To me the converging objects of the universe
      perpetually flow,
All are written to me, and I must get what the writing
      means.

And I know I am deathless,
I know this orbit of mine cannot be swept by a
      carpenter's compass,
I know I shall not pass like a child's carlacue cut with a
      burnt stick at night.

I know I am august,
I do not trouble my spirit to vindicate itself or be understood,
I see that the elementary laws never apologize,
I reckon I behave no prouder than the level I plant my
      house by after all.

I exist as I am, that is enough,
If no other in the world be aware I sit content,
And if each and all be aware I sit content.

One world is aware, and by far the largest to me, and
      that is myself,
And whether I come to my own today or in ten thousand
      or ten million years,
I can cheerfully take it now, or with equal cheerfulness
      I can wait.

My foothold is tenoned and mortised in granite,
I laugh at what you call dissolution,
And I know the amplitude of time.

   [21]
I am the poet of the body,
And I am the poet of the soul.

The pleasures of heaven are with me, and the pains of
      hell are with me,
The first I graft and increase upon myself . . . . the latter I
      translate into a new tongue.

I am the poet of the woman the same as the man,
And I say it is as great to be a woman as to be a man,
And I say there is nothing greater than the mother of men.

I chant a new chant of dilation or pride,
We have had ducking and deprecating about enough,
I show that size is only development.

Have you outstript the rest? Are you the President?
It is a trifle . . . . they will more than arrive there every one,
      and still pass on.

I am he that walks with the tender and growing night;
I call to the earth and sea half-held by the night.

Press close barebosomed night! Press close magnetic
      nourishing night!
Night of south winds! Night of the large few stars!
Still nodding night! Mad naked summer night!

Smile O voluptuous coolbreathed earth!
Earth of the slumbering and liquid trees!
Earth of departed sunset! Earth of the mountains misty-topt!
Earth of the vitreous pour of the full moon just tinged
      with blue!
Earth of shine and dark mottling the tide of the river!
Earth of the limpid gray of clouds brighter and clearer
      for my sake!
Far-swooping elbowed earth! Rich apple-blossomed earth!
Smile, for your lover comes!

Prodigal! you have given me love! .... therefore I
      to you give love!
O unspeakable passionate love!

Thruster holding me tight and that I hold tight!
We hurt each other as the bridegroom and the bride hurt
      each other.

[22]
You sea! I resign myself to you also .... I guess
      what you mean,
I behold from the beach your crooked inviting fingers,
I believe you refuse to go back without feeling of me;
We must have a turn together .... I undress .... hurry me
      out of sight of the land,
Cushion me soft .... rock me in billowy drowse,
Dash me with amorous wet .... I can repay you.

Sea of stretched ground-swells!
Sea breathing broad and convulsive breaths!
Sea of the brine of life! Sea of unshovelled and
     always-ready graves!
Howler and scooper of storms! Capricious and dainty sea!
I am integral with you . . . . I too am of one phase and
     of all phases.

Partaker of influx and efflux . . . . extoller of hate and
     conciliation,
Extoller of amies and those that sleep in each other's arms.

I am he attesting sympathy;
Shall I make my list of things in the house and skip
     the house that supports them?

I am the poet of commonsense and of the demonstrable
     and of immortality;
And am not the poet of goodness only . . . . I do not
     decline to be the poet of wickedness also.

Washes and razors for foofoos . . . . for me freckles and
     a bristling beard.

What blurt is it about virtue and about vice?
Evil propels me, and reform of evil propels me . . . .
     I stand indifferent,
My gait is no faultfinder's or rejector's gait,
I moisten the roots of all that has grown.

Did you fear some scrofula out of the unflagging pregnancy?
Did you guess the celestial laws are yet to be worked
     over and rectified?

I step up to say that what we do is right and what we
     affirm is right . . . . and some is only the ore of right,

Witnesses of us . . . . one side a balance and the antipodal
    side a balance,
This is the lexicographer or chemist . . . . this made a
    grammar of the old cartouches,
These mariners put the ship through dangerous
    unknown seas,
This is the geologist, and this works with the scalpel,
    and this is a mathematician.

Gentlemen I receive you, and attach and clasp hands
    with you,
The facts are useful and real . . . . they are not my
    dwelling . . . . I enter by them to an area of the dwelling.

I am less the reminder of property or qualities, and more
    the remainder of life,
Soft doctrine as steady help as stable doctrine,
Thoughts and deeds of the present our rouse and early start.

This minute that comes to me over the past decillions,
There is no better than it and now.

What behaved well in the past or behaves well today
    is not such a wonder,
The wonder is always and always how there can be a mean
    man or an infidel.

[23]
Endless unfolding of words of ages!
And mine a word of the modern . . . . a word en masse.

A word of the faith that never balks,
One time as good as another time . . . . here or
    henceforward it is all the same to me.

A word of reality . . . . materialism first and last imbuing.

Hurrah for positive science! Long live exact demonstration!
Fetch stonecrop and mix it with cedar and branches of lilac;
And go on the square for my own sake and for other's sake,
And make short account of neuters and geldings, and
      favor men and women fully equipped,
And beat the gong of revolt, and stop with fugitives
      and them that plot and conspire.

[24]

Walt Whitman, an American, one of the roughs, a kosmos,
Disorderly fleshy and sensual .... eating drinking and
      breeding,
No sentimentalist .... no stander above men and women or
      apart from them .... no more modest than immodest.

Unscrew the locks from the doors!
Unscrew the doors themselves from their jambs!

Whoever degrades another degrades me .... and whatever
      is done or said returns at last to me,
And whatever I do or say I also return.

Through me the afflatus surging and surging .... through
      me the current and index.

I speak the password primeval .... I give the sign of
      democracy;
By God! I will accept nothing which all cannot have
      their counterpart of on the same terms.

Through me many long dumb voices,
Voices of the interminable generations of slaves,
Voices of prostitutes and of deformed persons,
Voices of the diseased and despairing, and of thieves
      and dwarfs,
Voices of cycles of preparation and accretion,

And of the threads that connect the stars—and of wombs,
    and of the fatherstuff,
And of the rights of them the others are down upon,
Of the trivial and flat and foolish and despised,
Of fog in the air and beetles rolling balls of dung.

Through me forbidden voices,
Voices of sexes and lusts . . . . voices veiled, and I remove
    the veil,
Voices indecent by me clarified and transfigured.

I do not press my finger across my mouth,
I keep as delicate around the bowels as around the
    head and heart,
Copulation is no more rank to me than death is.

I believe in the flesh and the appetites,
Seeing hearing and feeling are miracles, and each part
    and tag of me is a miracle.

Divine am I inside and out, and I make holy whatever
    I touch or am touched from;
The scent of these arm-pits is aroma finer than prayer,
This head is more than churches or bibles or creeds.

If I worship any particular thing it shall be some of the
    spread of my body;
Translucent mould of me it shall be you,
Shaded ledges and rests, firm masculine coulter,
    it shall be you,

Whatever goes to the tilth of me it shall be you,
You my rich blood, your milky stream pale strippings
    of my life;
Breast that presses against other breasts it shall be you.
My brain it shall be your occult convolutions,
Root of washed sweet-flag, timorous pond-snipe, nest
    of guarded duplicate eggs, it shall be you,

Mixed tussled hay of head and beard and brawn
      it shall be you,
Trickling sap of maple, fibre of manly wheat, it shall be you;
Sun so generous it shall be you,
Vapors lighting and shading my face it shall be you,
You sweaty brooks and dews it shall be you.
Winds whose soft-tickling genitals rub against me
      it shall be you,
Broad muscular fields, branches of liveoak, loving
      lounger in my winding paths, it shall be you,
Hands I have taken, face I have kissed, mortal I have
      ever touched, it shall be you.

I dote on myself . . . . there is that lot of me, and all
      so luscious,
Each moment and whatever happens thrills me with joy.

I cannot tell how my ankles bend . . . . nor whence
      the cause of my faintest wish,
Nor the cause of the friendship I emit . . . . nor the cause
      of the friendship I take again.

To walk up my stoop is unaccountable . . . . I pause to
      consider if it really be,
That I eat and drink is spectacle enough for the great
      authors and schools,
A morning-glory at my window satisfies me more than the
      metaphysics of books.

To behold the daybreak!
The little light fades the immense and diaphanous shadows,
The air tastes good to my palate.

Hefts of the moving world at innocent gambols,
      silently rising, freshly exuding,
Scooting obliquely high and low.

Something I cannot see puts upward libidinous prongs,
Seas of bright juice suffuse heaven.

The earth by the sky staid with . . . . the daily close of
    their junction,
The heaved challenge from the east that moment
    over my head,
The mocking taunt, See then whether you shall be master!

   [25]
Dazzling and tremendous how quick the sunrise would
    kill me,
If I could not now and always send sunrise out of me.

We also ascend dazzling and tremendous as the sun,
We found our own my soul in the calm and cool of
    the daybreak.

My voice goes after what my eyes cannot reach,
With the twirl of my tongue I encompass worlds and
    volumes of worlds.

Speech is the twin of my vision . . . . it is unequal to
    measure itself.

It provokes me forever,
It says sarcastically, Walt, you understand enough . . . .
    why don't you let it out then?

Come now I will not be tantalized . . . . you conceive
    too much of articulation.

Do you not know how the buds beneath are folded?
Waiting in gloom protected by frost,
The dirt receding before my prophetical screams,
I underlying causes to balance them at last,

My knowledge my live parts . . . . it keeping tally with the
    meaning of things;
Happiness . . . . which whoever hears me let him or her
    set out in search of this day.

My final merit I refuse you . . . . I refuse putting from
    me the best I am.

Encompass worlds but never try to encompass me,
I crowd your noisiest talk by looking toward you.

Writing and talk do not prove me,
I carry the plenum of proof and every thing else in my face,
With the hush of my lips I confound the topmost skeptic.

[26]
I think I will do nothing for a long time but listen,
And accrue what I hear into myself . . . . and let sounds
    contribute toward me.

I hear the bravuras of birds . . . . the bustle of growing
    wheat . . . . gossip of flames . . . . clack of sticks
    cooking my meals.

I hear the sound of the human voice . . . . a sound I love,
I hear all sounds as they are tuned to their uses . . . .
    sounds of the city and sounds out of the city . . . .
    sounds of the day and night;
Talkative young ones to those that like them . . . . the
    recitative of fish-pedlars and fruit-pedlars . . . . the
    loud laugh of workpeople at their meals,
The angry base of disjointed friendship . . . . the faint
    tones of the sick,
The judge with hands tight to the desk, his shaky lips
    pronouncing a death-sentence,
The heave'e'yo of stevedores unlading ships by the
    wharves . . . . the refrain of the anchor-lifters;

The ring of alarm-bells .... the cry of fire .... the
    whirr of swift-streaking engines and hose-carts with
    premonitory tinkles and colored lights,
The steam-whistle .... the solid roll of the train of
    approaching cars;
The slow-march played at night at the head of the
    association,
They go to guard some corpse .... the flag-tops are
    draped with black muslin.

I hear the violincello or man's heart complaint,
And hear the keyed cornet or else the echo of sunset.

I hear the chorus .... it is a grand-opera .... this indeed
    is music!

A tenor large and fresh as the creation fills me,
The orbic flex of his mouth is pouring and filling me full.

I hear the trained soprano .... she convulses me like
    the climax of my love-grip;
The orchestra whirls me wider than Uranus flies,
It wrenches unnamable ardors from my breast,
It throbs me to gulps of the farthest down horror,
It sails me .... I dab with bare feet .... they are licked
    by the indolent waves,
I am exposed .... cut by bitter and poisoned hail,
Steeped amid honeyed morphine .... my windpipe
    squeezed in the fakes of death,
Let up again to feel the puzzle of puzzles,
And that we call Being.

[27]
To be in any form, what is that?
If nothing lay more developed the quahaug and its callous
    shell were enough.

Mine is no callous shell,
I have instant conductors all over me whether I pass or stop,
They seize every object and lead it harmlessly through me.
I merely stir, press, feel with my fingers, and am happy,
To touch my person to some one else's is about as much as
     I can stand.

[28]
Is this then a touch? .... quivering me to a new identity,
Flames and ether making a rush for my veins,
Treacherous tip of me reaching and crowding to help them,
My flesh and blood playing out lightning, to strike what
     is hardly different from myself,
On all sides prurient provokers stiffening my limbs,
Straining the udder of my heart for its withheld drip,
Behaving licentious towards me, taking no denial,
Depriving me of my best as for a purpose,
Unbuttoning my clothes and holding me by the bare waist,
Deluding my confusion with the calm of the sunlight
     and pasture fields,
Immodestly sliding the fellow-senses away,
They bribed to swap off with touch, and go and graze
     at the edges of me,
No consideration, no regard for my draining strength or
     my anger,
Fetching the rest of the herd around to enjoy them awhile,
Then all uniting to stand on a headland and worry me.

The sentries desert every other part of me,
They have left me helpless to a red marauder,
They all come to the headland to witness and assist
     against me.

I am given up by traitors;
I talk wildly .... I have lost my wits .... I and nobody else
     am the greatest traitor,

I went myself first to the headland . . . . my own hands
    carried me there.

You villain touch! what are you doing? . . . . my breath
    is tight in its throat;
Unclench your floodgates! you are too much for me.

[29]
Blind loving wrestling touch! Sheathed hooded
    sharptoothed touch!
Did it make you ache so leaving me?

Parting tracked by arriving . . . . perpetual payment of the
    perpetual loan,
Rich showering rain, and recompense richer afterward.

Sprouts take and accumulate . . . . stand by the curb
    prolific and vital,
Landscapes projected masculine full-sized and golden.

[30]
All truths wait in all things,
They neither hasten their own delivery nor resist it,
They do not need the obstetric forceps of the surgeon,
The insignificant is as big to me as any,
What is less or more than a touch?

Logic and sermons never convince,
The damp of the night drives deeper into my soul.

Only what proves itself to every man and woman is so,
Only what nobody denies is so.

A minute and a drop of me settle my brain;
I believe the soggy clods shall become lovers and lamps,
And a compend of compends is the meat of a man or woman.

And a summit and flower there is the feeling they have
    for each other,
And they are to branch boundlessly out of that lesson
    until it becomes omnific,
And until every one shall delight us, and we them.

[31]

I believe a leaf of grass is no less than the journeywork of
    the stars,
And the pismire is equally perfect, and a grain of sand,
    and the egg of the wren,
And the tree-toad is a chef-d'œuvre for the highest,
And the running blackberry would adorn the parlors of
    heaven,
And the narrowest hinge in my hand puts to scorn all
    machinery,
And the cow crunching with depressed head surpasses
    any statue,
And a mouse is miracle enough to stagger sextillions of infidels,
And I could come every afternoon of my life to look at the
    farmer's girl boiling her iron tea-kettle and baking shortcake.

I find I incorporate gneiss and coal and long-threaded moss
    and fruits and grains and esculent roots,
And am stucco'd with quadrupeds and birds all over,
And have distanced what is behind me for good reasons,
And call any thing close again when I desire it.

In vain the speeding or shyness,
In vain the plutonic rocks send their old heat against my approach,
In vain the mastodon retreats beneath its own powdered bones,
In vain objects stand leagues off and assume manifold shapes,
In vain the ocean settling in hollows and the great monsters
    lying low,
In vain the buzzard houses herself with the sky,

In vain the snake slides through the creepers and logs,
In vain the elk takes to the inner passes of the woods,
In vain the razorbilled auk sails far north to Labrador,
I follow quickly .... I ascend to the nest in the fissure of
    the cliff.

[32]
I think I could turn and live awhile with the animals ....
    they are so placid and self-contained,
I stand and look at them sometimes half the day long.

They do not sweat and whine about their condition,
They do not lie awake in the dark and weep for their sins,
They do not make me sick discussing their duty to God,
Not one is dissatisfied .... not one is demented with the
    mania of owning things,
Not one kneels to another nor to his kind that lived
    thousands of years ago,
Not one is respectable or industrious over the whole earth.

So they show their relations to me and I accept them;
They bring me tokens of myself .... they evince them plainly
    in their possession.

I do not know where they got those tokens,
I must have passed that way untold times ago and
    negligently dropt them,
Myself moving forward then and now and forever,
Gathering and showing more always and with velocity,
Infinite and omnigenous and the like of these among them;
Not too exclusive toward the reachers of my remembrancers,
Picking out here one that shall be my amie,
Choosing to go with him on brotherly terms.

A gigantic beauty of a stallion, fresh and responsive to my
    caresses,
Head high in the forehead and wide between the ears,
Limbs glossy and supple, tail dusting the ground,
Eyes well apart and full of sparkling wickedness . . . . ears
    finely cut and flexibly moving.

His nostrils dilate . . . . my heels embrace him . . . . his well
    built limbs tremble with pleasure . . . . we speed
    around and return.

I but use you a moment and then I resign you stallion . . . .
    and do not need your paces, and outgallop them,
And myself as I stand or sit pass faster than you.

    [33]
Swift wind! Space! My Soul! Now I know it is true what I
    guessed at;
What I guessed when I loafed on the grass,
What I guessed while I lay alone in my bed . . . . and again as I
    walked the beach under the paling stars of the morning.

My ties and ballasts leave me . . . . I travel . . . . I sail . . . .
    my elbows rest in the sea-gaps,
I skirt the sierras . . . . my palms cover continents,
I am afoot with my vision.

By the city's quadrangular houses . . . . in log-huts, or
    camping with lumbermen,
Along the ruts of the turnpike . . . . along the dry gulch and
    rivulet bed,
Hoeing my onion-patch, and rows of carrots and parsnips
    . . . . crossing savannas . . . . trailing in forests,
Prospecting . . . . gold-digging . . . . girdling the trees of
    a new purchase,
Scorched ankle-deep by the hot sand . . . . hauling my boat
    down the shallow river;

Where the panther walks to and fro on a limb overhead
   .... where the buck turns furiously at the hunter,
Where the rattlesnake suns his flabby length on a rock ....
   where the otter is feeding on fish,
Where the alligator in his tough pimples sleeps by the bayou,
Where the black bear is searching for roots or honey ....
   where the beaver pats the mud with his paddle-tail;
Over the growing sugar .... over the cottonplant .... over
   the rice in its low moist field;
Over the sharp-peaked farmhouse with its scalloped scum
   and slender shoots from the gutters;
Over the western persimmon .... over the longleaved
   corn and the delicate blue-flowered flax;
Over the white and brown buckwheat, a hummer and
   a buzzer there with the rest.

Over the dusky green of the rye as it ripples and shades in
   the breeze;
Scaling mountains .... pulling myself cautiously up ....
   holding on by low scragged limbs,
Walking the path worn in the grass and beat through the
   leaves of the brush;
Where the quail is whistling betwixt the woods and the
   wheatlot,
Where the bat flies in the July eve .... where the great
   goldbug drops through the dark;
Where the flails keep time on the barn floor,
Where the brook puts out of the roots of the old tree and
   flows to the meadow,
Where cattle stand and shake away flies with the tremulous
   shuddering of their hides,
Where the cheese-cloth hangs in the kitchen, and andirons
   straddle the hearth-slab, and cobwebs fall in festoons
   from the rafters;
Where triphammers crash .... where the press is whirling
   its cylinders;

Wherever the human heart beats with terrible throes out
    of its ribs;
Where the pear-shaped balloon is floating aloft. . . .
    floating in it myself and looking composedly down;
Where the life-car is drawn on the slipnoose . . . . where the
    heat hatches pale-green eggs in the dented sand,
Where the she-whale swims with her calves and never
    forsakes them,
Where the steamship trails hindways its long pennant of
    smoke,
Where the ground-shark's fin cuts like a black chip
    out of the water,
Where the half-burned brig is riding on unknown currents,
Where shells grow to her slimy deck, and the dead are
    corrupting below;
Where the striped and starred flag is borne at the head of the
    regiments;
Approaching Manhattan, up by the long-stretching island,
Under Niagara, the cataract falling like a veil over my
    countenance;
Upon a door-step . . . . upon the horse-block of hard wood
    outside,
Upon the race-course, or enjoying pic-nics or jigs or a
    good game of base-ball,
At he-festivals with blackguard jibes and ironical license
    and bull-dances and drinking and laughter,
At the cider-mill, tasting the sweet of the brown sqush
    . . . . sucking the juice through a straw,
At apple-peelings, wanting kisses for all the red fruit I find,
At musters and beach-parties and friendly bees and
    huskings and house-raisings;
Where the mockingbird sounds his delicious gurgles, and
    cackles and screams and weeps,
Where the hay-rick stands in the barnyard, and the
    dry-stalks are scattered, and the brood cow waits
    in the hovel,

Where the bull advances to do his masculine work, and the
stud to the mare, and the cock is treading the hen,
Where the heifers browse, and the geese nip their food
with short jerks;
Where the sundown shadows lengthen over the limitless
and lonesome prairie,
Where the herds of buffalo make a crawling spread of
the square miles far and near;
Where the hummingbird shimmers .... where the neck
of the longlived swan is curving and winding;
Where the laughing-gull scoots by the slappy shore and
laughs her near-human laugh;
Where beehives range on a gray bench in the garden
half-hid by the high weeds;
Where the band-necked partridges roost in a ring on the
ground with their heads out;
Where burial coaches enter the arched gates of a cemetery;
Where winter wolves bark amid wastes of snow and icicled
trees;
Where the yellow-crowned heron comes to the edge of the
marsh at night and feeds upon small crabs;
Where the splash of swimmers and divers cools the
warm noon;
Where the katydid works her chromatic reed on the
walnut-tree over the well;
Through patches of citrons and cucumbers with silver-wired
leaves,
Through the salt-lick or orange glade .... or under conical firs;
Through the gymnasium .... through the curtained
saloon .... through the office or public hall;
Pleased with the native and pleased with the foreign ....
pleased with the new and old,
Pleased with women, the homely as well as the handsome,
Pleased with the quakeress as she puts off her bonnet and
talks melodiously,

Pleased with the primitive tunes of the choir of the
    whitewashed church,
Pleased with the earnest words of the sweating Methodist
    preacher, or any preacher . . . . looking seriously
    at the camp-meeting;
Looking in at the shop-windows in Broadway the whole
    forenoon . . . . pressing the flesh of my nose to the
    thick plate-glass,
Wandering the same afternoon with my face turned up
    to the clouds;
My right and left arms round the sides of two friends and
    I in the middle;
Coming home with the bearded and dark-cheeked bush-boy
    . . . . riding behind him at the drape of the day;
Far from the settlements studying the print of animals'
    feet, or the moccasin print;
By the cot in the hospital reaching lemonade to a
    feverish patient,
By the coffined corpse when all is still, examining with
    a candle;
Voyaging to every port to dicker and adventure;
Hurrying with the modern crowd, as eager and fickle as any,
Hot toward one I hate, ready in my madness to knife him;
Solitary at midnight in my back yard, my thoughts gone
    from me a long while,
Walking the old hills of Judea with the beautiful gentle
    god by my side;
Speeding through space . . . . speeding through heaven and
    the stars,
Speeding amid the seven satellites and the broad ring and
    the diameter of eighty thousand miles,
Speeding with tailed meteors . . . . throwing fire-balls
    like the rest,
Carrying the crescent child that carries its own full mother
    in its belly:
Storming enjoying planning loving cautioning,

Backing and filling; appearing and disappearing,
I tread day and night such roads.

I visit the orchards of God and look at the spheric product,
And look at quintillions ripened, and look at quintillions
    green.

I fly the flight of the fluid and swallowing soul,
My course runs below the soundings of plummets.

I help myself to material and immaterial,
No guard can shut me off, no law can prevent me.

I anchor my ship for a little while only,
My messengers continually cruise away or bring their
    returns to me.

I go hunting polar furs and the seal . . . . leaping chasms
    with a pike-pointed staff . . . . clinging to topples of
    brittle and blue.

I ascend to the foretruck . . . . I take my place late at night
    in the crow's nest . . . . we sail through the arctic sea
    . . . . it is plenty light enough,
Through the clear atmosphere I stretch around on the
    wonderful beauty,
The enormous masses of ice pass me and I pass them . . . .
    the scenery is plain in all directions,
The white-topped mountains point up in the distance . . . .
    I fling out my fancies toward them;
We are about approaching some great battlefield in which
    we are soon to be engaged,
We pass the colossal outposts of the encampment . . . .
    we pass with still feet and caution;
Or we are entering by the suburbs some vast and ruined
    city . . . . the blocks and fallen architecture more
    than all the living cities of the globe.

I am a free companion . . . . I bivouac by invading watchfires.

I turn the bridegroom out of bed and stay with the bride
    myself,
And tighten her all night to my thighs and lips.

My voice is the wife's voice, the screech by the rail of
    the stairs,
They fetch my man's body up dripping and drowned.

I understand the large hearts of heroes,
The courage of present times and all times;
How the skipper saw the crowded and rudderless wreck
    of the steamship, and death chasing it up and down
    the storm,
How he knuckled tight and gave not back one inch, and was
    faithful of days and faithful of nights,
And chalked in large letters on a board, Be of good cheer,
    We will not desert you;
How he saved the drifting company at last,
How the lank loose-gowned women looked when boated
    from the side of their prepared graves,
How the silent old-faced infants, and the lifted sick, and
    the sharplipped unshaved men;
All this I swallow and it tastes good . . . . I like it well,
    and it becomes mine,
I am the man . . . . I suffered . . . . I was there.

The disdain and calmness of martyrs,
The mother condemned for a witch and burnt with dry
    wood, and her children gazing on;
The hounded slave that flags in the race and leans by the
    fence, blowing and covered with sweat,
The twinges that sting like needles his legs and neck,
The murderous buckshot and the bullets,
All these I feel or am.

I am the hounded slave . . . . I wince at the bite of the dogs,
Hell and despair are upon me . . . . crack and again crack
     the marksmen,
I clutch the rails of the fence . . . . my gore dribs thinned
     with the ooze of my skin,
I fall on the weeds and stones,
The riders spur their unwilling horses and haul close,
They taunt my dizzy ears . . . . they beat me violently
     over the head with their whip-stocks.

Agonies are one of my changes of garments;
I do not ask the wounded person how he feels . . . . I myself
     become the wounded person,
My hurt turns livid upon me as I lean on a cane and observe.

I am the mashed fireman with breastbone broken . . . .
     tumbling walls buried me in their debris,
Heat and smoke I inspired . . . . I heard the yelling shouts
     of my comrades,
I heard the distant click of their picks and shovels;
They have cleared the beams away . . . . they tenderly
     lift me forth.

I lie in the night air in my red shirt . . . . the pervading
     hush is for my sake,
Painless after all I lie, exhausted but not so unhappy,
White and beautiful are the faces around me . . . . the
     heads are bared of their fire-caps,
The kneeling crowd fades with the light of the torches.

Distant and dead resuscitate,
They show as the dial or move as the hands of me . . . . and
     I am the clock myself.
I am an old artillerist, and tell of some fort's bombardment
     . . . . and am there again.

Again the reveille of drummers . . . . again the attacking
    cannon and mortars and howitzers,
Again the attacked send their cannon responsive.

I take part . . . . I see and hear the whole,
The cries and curses and roar . . . . the plaudits for well
    aimed shots,
The ambulanza slowly passing and trailing its red drip,
Workmen searching after damages and to make
    indispensable repairs,
The fall of grenades through the rent roof . . . . the fan-shaped
    explosion,
The whizz of limbs heads stone wood and iron high in the air.

Again gurgles the mouth of my dying general . . . . he
    furiously waves with his hand,
He gasps through the clot . . . . Mind not me . . . . mind . . . .
    the entrenchments.

    [34]
I tell not the fall of Alamo . . . . not one escaped to tell
    the fall of Alamo,
The hundred and fifty are dumb yet at Alamo.

Hear now the tale of a jetblack sunrise,
Hear of the murder in cold blood of four hundred and twelve
    young men.

Retreating they had formed in a hollow square with their
    baggage for breastworks,
Nine hundred lives out of the surrounding enemy's nine
    times their number was the price they took in advance,
Their colonel was wounded and their ammunition gone,
They treated for an honorable capitulation, received
    writing and seal, gave up their arms, and marched back
    prisoners of war.

They were the glory of the race of rangers,
Matchless with a horse, a rifle, a song, a supper or a courtship,
Large, turbulent, brave, handsome, generous, proud and
    affectionate,
Bearded, sunburnt, dressed in the free costume of hunters,
Not a single one over thirty years of age.

The second Sunday morning they were brought out in
    squads and massacred . . . . it was beautiful early
    summer,
The work commenced about five o'clock and was over
    by eight.

None obeyed the command to kneel,
Some made a mad and helpless rush . . . . some stood stark
    and straight,
A few fell at once, shot in the temple or heart . . . . the living
    and dead lay together,
The maimed and mangled dug in the dirt . . . . the
    new-comers saw them there;
Some half-killed attempted to crawl away,
These were dispatched with bayonets or battered with the
    blunts of muskets;
A youth not seventeen years old seized his assassin till
    two more came to release him,
The three were all torn, and covered with the boy's blood.

At eleven o'clock began the burning of the bodies;
And that is the tale of the murder of the four hundred
    and twelve young men,
And that was a jetblack sunrise.

[35]
Did you read in the seabooks of the oldfashioned
    frigate-fight?
Did you learn who won by the light of the moon and stars?

Our foe was no skulk in his ship, I tell you,
His was the English pluck, and there is no tougher or truer,
    and never was, and never will be;
Along the lowered eve he came, horribly raking us.

We closed with him . . . . the yards entangled . . . . the cannon
    touched,
My captain lashed fast with his own hands.

We had received some eighteen-pound shots under the
    water,
On our lower-gun-deck two large pieces had burst at the first
    fire, killing all around and blowing up overhead.

Ten o'clock at night, and the full moon shining and the
    leaks on the gain, and five feet of water reported,
The master-at-arms loosing the prisoners confined in the
    after-hold to give them a chance for themselves.

The transit to and from the magazine was now stopped
    by the sentinels,
They saw so many strange faces they did not know whom
    to trust.

Our frigate was afire . . . . the other asked if we demanded
    quarters? if our colors were struck and the fighting done?

I laughed content when I heard the voice of my little
    captain,
We have not struck, he composedly cried, We have just
    begun our part of the fighting.

Only three guns were in use,
One was directed by the captain himself against the enemy's
    mainmast,
Two well-served with grape and canister silenced his
    musketry and cleared his decks.

The tops alone seconded the fire of this little battery,
    especially the maintop,
They all held out bravely during the whole of the action.

Not a moment's cease,
The leaks gained fast on the pumps .... the fire eat
    toward the powder-magazine,
One of the pumps was shot away .... it was generally
    thought we were sinking.

Serene stood the little captain,
He was not hurried .... his voice was neither high nor low,
His eyes gave more light to us than our battle-lanterns.

Toward twelve at night, there in the beams of the moon
    they surrendered to us.

[36]

Stretched and still lay the midnight,
Two great hulls motionless on the breast of the darkness,
Our vessel riddled and slowly sinking .... preparations
    to pass to the one we had conquered,
The captain on the quarter deck coldly giving his
    orders through a countenance white as a sheet,
Near by the corpse of the child that served in the cabin,
The dead face of an old salt with long white hair and
    carefully curled whiskers,
The flames spite of all that could be done flickering
    aloft and below,
The husky voices of the two or three officers yet
    fit for duty,
Formless stacks of bodies and bodies by themselves ....
    dabs of flesh upon the masts and spars,
The cut of cordage and dangle of rigging .... the slight
    shock of the soothe of waves,

Black and impassive guns, and litter of powder-parcells, and
    the strong scent,
Delicate sniffs of the seabreeze . . . . smells of sedgy
    grass and fields by the shore . . . . death-messages given
    in charge to survivors,
The hiss of the surgeon's knife and the gnawing teeth
    of his saw,
The wheeze, the cluck, the swash of falling blood . . . . the
    short wild scream, the long dull tapering groan,
These so . . . . these irretrievable.

   [37]
O Christ! My fit is mastering me!
What the rebel said gaily adjusting his throat to
    the rope-noose,
What the savage at the stump, his eye-sockets empty,
    his mouth spirting whoops and defiance,
What stills the traveler come to the vault at Mount Vernon,
What sobers the Brooklyn boy as he looks down the shores
    of the Wallabout and remembers the prison ships,
What burnt the guns of the redcoat at Saratoga when
    he surrendered his brigades,
These become mine and me every one, and they are
    but little,
I become as much more as I like.

I become any presence or truth of humanity here,
And see myself in prison shaped like another man,
And feel the dull unintermitted pain.

For me the keepers of convicts shoulder their carbines
    and keep watch,
It is I let out in the morning and barred at night.

Not a mutineer walks handcuffed to the jail, but I am
    handcuffed to him and walk by his side.

I am less the jolly one there, and more the silent one
    with sweat on my twitching lips.

Not a youngster is taken for larceny, but I go too and am
    tried and sentenced.

Not a cholera patient lies at the last gasp, but I also
    lie at the last gasp,
My face is ash-colored, my sinews gnarl .... away from
    me people retreat.

Askers embody themselves in me, and I am embodied
    in them,
I project my hat and sit shamefaced and beg.

I rise extatic through all, and sweep with the true gravitation,
The whirling and whirling is elemental within me.

[38]
Somehow I have been stunned. Stand back!
Give me a little time beyond my cuffed head and slumbers
    and dreams and gaping,
I discover myself on a verge of the usual mistake.

That I could forget the mockers and insults!
That I could forget the trickling tears and the blows of the
    bludgeons and hammers!
That I could look with a separate look on my own
    crucifixion and bloody crowning!

I remember .... I resume the overstaid fraction,
The grave of rock multiplies what has been confided to it
    .... or to any graves,
The corpses rise .... the gashes heal .... the fastenings
    roll away.

I troop forth replenished with supreme power, one of an
    average unending procession,
We walk the roads of Ohio and Massachusetts and
    Virginia and Wisconsin and New York and New Orleans
    and Texas and Montreal and San Francisco and
    Charleston and Savannah and Mexico,
Inland and by the seacoast and boundary lines . . . . and we
    pass the boundary lines.

Our swift ordinances are on their way over the whole earth,
The blossoms we wear in our hats are the growth of
    two thousand years.

Eleves I salute you,
I see the approach of your numberless gangs . . . . I see
    you understand yourselves and me,
And know that they who have eyes are divine, and the
    blind and lame are equally divine,
And that my steps drag behind yours yet go before them,
And are aware how I am with you no more than I am
    with everybody.

[39]
The friendly and flowing savage . . . . Who is he?
Is he waiting for civilization or past it and mastering it?

Is he some southwesterner raised outdoors? Is he Canadian?
Is he from the Mississippi country? or from Iowa, Oregon
    or California? or from the mountain? or prairie
    life or bush-life? or from the sea?

Wherever he goes men and women accept and desire him,
They desire he should like them and touch them and
    speak to them and stay with them.

Behaviour lawless as snow-flakes .... words simple as
    grass .... uncombed head and laughter and naivete;
Slowstepping feet and the common features, and the
    common modes and emanations,
They descend in new forms from the tips of his fingers,
They are wafted with the odor of his body or breath ....
    they fly out of the glance of his eyes.

[40]
Flaunt of the sunshine I need not your bask .... lie over,
You light surfaces only .... I force the surfaces and
    the depths also.

Earth! you seem to look for something at my hands,
Say old topknot! what do you want?

Man or woman! I might tell how I like you, but cannot,
And might tell what it is in me and what it is in you,
    but cannot,
And might tell the pinings I have .... the pulse of my
    nights and days.

Behold I do not give lectures or a little charity,
What I give I give out of myself.

You there, impotent, loose in the knees, open your
    scarfed chops till I blow grit within you,
Spread your palms and lift the flaps of your pockets,
I am not to be denied .... I compel .... I have stores plenty
    and to spare,
And any thing I have I bestow.

I do not ask who you are .... that is not important to me,
You can do nothing and be nothing but what I will
    infold you.

To a drudge of the cottonfields or emptier of privies
    I lean .... on his right cheek I put the family kiss,
And in my soul I swear I never will deny him.

On women fit for conception I start bigger and
    nimbler babes,
This day I am jetting the stuff of far more arrogant republics.

To any one dying .... thither I speed and twist the knob of
    the door,
Turn the bedclothes toward the foot of the bed,
Let the physician and the priest go home.

I seize the descending man .... I raise him with
    resistless will.

O despairer, here is my neck,
By God! you shall not go down! Hang your whole weight
    upon me.

I dilate you with tremendous breath .... I buoy you up;
Every room of the house do I fill with an armed force
    .... lovers of me bafflers of graves:
Sleep! I and they keep guard all night;
Not doubt, not decease shall dare to lay finger upon you,
I have embraced you, and henceforth possess you
    to myself,
And when you rise in the morning you will find what I tell
    you is so.

   [41]
I am he bringing help for the sick as they pant on their backs,
And for strong upright men I bring yet more needed help.

I heard what was said of the universe,
Heard it and heard of several thousand years;

It is middling well as far as it goes .... but is that all?

Magnifying and applying come I,
Outbidding at the start the old cautious hucksters,
The most they offer for mankind and eternity less than a
    spirt of my own seminal wet,
Taking myself the exact dimensions of Jehovah and laying
    them away,
Lithographing Kronos and Zeus his son, and Hercules
    his grandson,
Buying drafts of Osiris and Isis and Belus and Brahma
    and Adonai,
In my portfolio placing Manito loose, and Allah on a
    leaf, and the crucifix engraved,
With Odin, and the hideous-faced Mexitli, and all idols
    and images,
Honestly taking them all for what they are worth, and not
    a cent more,
Admitting they were alive and did the work of their day,
Admitting they bore mites as for unfledged birds
    who have now to rise and fly and sing for themselves,
Accepting the rough deific sketches to fill out better
    in myself . . . . bestowing them freely on each man
    and woman I see,
Discovering as much or more in a framer framing a house,
Putting higher claims for him there with his rolled-up
    sleeves, driving the mallet and chisel;
Not objecting to special revelations . . . . considering a
    curl of smoke or a hair on the back of my hand as
    curious as any revelation;
Those ahold of fire-engines and hook-and-ladder ropes
    more to me than the gods of the antique wars,
Minding their voices peal through the crash of destruction,
Their brawny limbs passing safe over charred laths . . . . their
    white foreheads whole and unhurt out of the flames;
By the mechanic's wife with her babe at her nipple
    interceding for every person born;

Three scythes at harvest whizzing in a row from three
    lusty angels with shirts bagged out at their waists;
The snag-toothed hostler with red hair redeeming sins past
    and to come,
Selling all he possesses and traveling on foot to fee
    lawyers for his brother and sit by him while he is
    tried for forgery:
What was strewn in the amplest strewing the square rod
    about me, and not filling the square rod then;
The bull and the bug never worshipped half enough,
Dung and dirt more admirable than was dreamed,
The supernatural of no account . . . . myself waiting my
    time to be one of the supremes,
The day getting ready for me when I shall do as much good
    as the best, and be as prodigious,
Guessing when I am it will not tickle me much to receive
    puffs out of pulpit or print;
By my life-lumps! becoming already a creator!

Putting myself here and now to the ambushed womb
    of the shadows!

[42]
. . . . A call in the midst of the crowd,
My own voice, orotund sweeping and final.

Come my children,
Come my boys and girls, and my women and household
    and intimates,
Now the performer launches his nerve . . . . he has passed
    his prelude on the reeds within.

Easily written loosefingered chords! I feel the thrum
    of their climax and close.

My head evolves on my neck,
Music rolls, but not from the organ . . . . folks are around
    me, but they are no household of mine.

Ever the hard and unsunk ground,
Ever the eaters and drinkers . . . . ever the upward and
    downward sun . . . . ever the air and the ceaseless tides,
Ever myself and my neighbors, refreshing and wicked
    and real,
Ever the old inexplicable query . . . . ever that thorned
    thumb—that breath of itches and thirsts,
Ever the vexer's hoot! hoot! till we find where the sly
    one hides and bring him forth;
Ever love . . . . ever the sobbing liquid of life,
Ever the bandage under the chin . . . . ever the trestles
    of death.

Here and there with dimes on the eyes walking,
To feed the greed of the belly the brains liberally spooning,
Tickets buying or taking or selling, but in to the feast
    never once going;
Many sweating and ploughing and thrashing, and then the
    chaff for payment receiving,
A few idly owning, and they the wheat continually
    claiming.

This is the city . . . . and I am one of the citizens;
Whatever interests the rest interests me . . . . politics,
    churches, newspapers, schools,
Benevolent societies, improvements, banks, tariffs,
    steamships, factories, markets,
Stocks and stores and real estate and personal estate.

They who piddle and patter here in collars and tailed
    coats . . . . I am aware who they are . . . . and that they
    are not worms or fleas,

I acknowledge the duplicates of myself under all the
    scrape-lipped and pipe-legged concealments.

The weakest and shallowest is deathless with me,
What I do and say the same waits for them,
Every thought that flounders in me the same flounders
    in them.

I know perfectly well my own egotism,
And know my omnivorous words, and cannot say any less,
And would fetch you whoever you are flush with myself.

My words are words of a questioning, and to indicate
    reality;
This printed and bound book.... but the printer and the
    printing-office boy?
The marriage estate and settlement.... but the body
    and mind of the bridegroom? also those of the bride?
The panorama of the sea.... but the sea itself?
The well-taken photographs.... but your wife or friend
    close and solid in your arms?
The fleet of ships of the line and all the modern
    improvements.... but the craft and pluck of the
    admiral?
The dishes and fare and furniture.... but the host and
    hostess, and the look out of their eyes?
The sky up there.... yet here or next door or across
    the way?
The saints and sages in history.... but you yourself?
Sermons and creeds and theology.... but the human
    brain, and what is called reason, and what is called
    love, and what is called life?

    [43]
I do not despise you priests;
My faith is the greatest of faiths and the least of faiths,

Enclosing all worship ancient and modern, and all
between ancient and modern,
Believing I shall come again upon the earth after
five thousand years,
Waiting responses from oracles .... honoring the gods ....
saluting the sun,
Making a fetish of the first rock or stump .... powowing
with sticks in the circle of obis,
Helping the lama or brahmin as he trims the lamps
of the idols,
Dancing yet through the streets in a phallic procession
.... rapt and austere in the woods, a gymnosophist,
Drinking mead from the skull-up .... to shasta and
vedas admirant .... minding the koran,
Walking the teokallis, spotted with gore from the stone
and knife—beating the serpent-skin drum;
Accepting the gospels, accepting him that was crucified,
knowing assuredly that he is divine,
To the mass kneeling—to the puritan's prayer rising—
sitting patiently in a pew,
Ranting and frothing in my insane crisis—waiting dead-like
till my spirit arouses me;
Looking forth on pavement and land, and outside of
pavement and land,
Belonging to the winders of the circuit of circuits.

One of that centripetal and centrifugal gang,
I turn and talk like a man leaving charges before a journey.

Down-hearted doubters, dull and excluded,
Frivolous sullen moping angry affected disheartened
atheistical,
I know every one of you, and know the unspoken
interrogatories,
By experience I know them.

How the flukes splash!
How they contort rapid as lightning, with spasms and spouts
    of blood!

Be at peace bloody flukes of doubters and sullen mopers,
I take my place among you as much as among any;
The past is the push of you and me and all precisely the same,
And the day and night are for you and me and all,
And what is yet untried and afterward is for you and me
    and all.

I do not know what is untried and afterward,
But I know it is sure and alive and sufficient.

Each who passes is considered, and each who stops is
    considered, and not a single one can it fail.

It cannot fail the young man who died and was buried,
Nor the young woman who died and was put by his side,
Nor the little child that peeped in at the door and then drew
    back and was never seen again,
Nor the old man who has lived without purpose, and feels
    it with bitterness worse than gall,
Nor him in the poorhouse tubercled by rum and the bad
    disorder,
Nor the numberless slaughtered and wrecked . . . . nor the
    brutish koboo, called the ordure of humanity,
Nor the sacs merely floating with open mouths for food
    to slip in,
Nor any thing in the earth, or down in the oldest graves
    of the earth,
Nor any thing in the myriads of spheres, nor one of the
    myriads of myriads that inhabit them,
Nor the present, nor the least wisp that is known.

It is time to explain myself . . . . let us stand up.

What is known I strip away . . . . I launch all men and
women forward with me into the unknown.

The clock indicates the moment . . . . but what does
eternity indicate?

Eternity lies in bottomless reservoirs . . . . its buckets are
rising forever and ever,
They pour and they pour and they exhale away.

We have thus far exhausted trillions of winters and summers;
There are trillions ahead, and trillions ahead of them.

Births have brought us richness and variety,
And other births will bring us richness and variety.

I do not call one greater and one smaller,
That which fills its period and place is equal to any.

Were mankind murderous or jealous upon you my brother
or my sister?
I am sorry for you . . . . they are not murderous or jealous
upon me;
All has been gentle with me . . . . I keep no account with
lamentation;
What have I to do with lamentation?

I am an acme of things accomplished, and I an encloser
of things to be.

My feet strike an apex of the apices of the stairs,
On every step bunches of ages, and larger bunches between
the steps,
All below duly traveled—and still I mount and mount.

Rise after rise bow the phantoms behind me,
Afar down I see the huge first Nothing, the vapor from
    the nostrils of death,
I know I was even there .... I waited unseen and always,
And slept while God carried me through the lethargic mist,
And took my time .... and took no hurt from the fœtid
    carbon.

Long I was hugged close .... long and long.

Immense have been the preparations for me,
Faithful and friendly the arms that have helped me.

Cycles ferried my cradle, rowing and rowing like cheerful
    boatmen;
For room to me stars kept aside in their own rings,
They sent influences to look after what was to hold me.

Before I was born out of my mother generations guided me,
My embryo has never been torpid .... nothing could
    overlay it;
For it the nebula cohered to an orb .... the long slow
    strata piled to rest it on .... vast vegetables gave it
    sustenance,
Monstrous sauroids transported it in their mouths and
    deposited it with care.

All forces have been steadily employed to complete and
    delight me,
Now I stand on this spot with my soul.

    [45]
Span of youth! Ever-pushed elasticity! Manhood balanced
    and florid and full!

My lovers suffocate me!
Crowding my lips, and thick in the pores of my skin,
Jostling me through streets and public halls .... coming
    naked to me at night,
Crying by day Ahoy from the rocks of the river ....
    swinging and chirping over my head,
Calling my name from flowerbeds or vines or tangled
    underbrush,
Or while I swim in the bath .... or drink from the pump
    at the corner .... or the curtain is down at the opera
    .... or I glimpse at a woman's face in the railroad car;
Lighting on every moment of my life,
Bussing my body with soft and balsamic busses,
Noiselessly passing handfuls out of their hearts and giving
    them to be mine.

Old age superbly rising! Ineffable grace of dying days!

Every condition promulges not only itself .... it promulges
    what grows after and out of itself,
And the dark hush promulges as much as any.

I open my scuttle at night and see the far-sprinkled systems,
And all I see, multiplied as high as I can cipher, edge but
    the rim of the farther systems.

Wider and wider they spread, expanding and always
    expanding.
Outward and outward and forever outward.

My sun has his sun, and round him obediently wheels,
He joins with his partners a group of superior circuit,
And greater sets follow, making specks of the greatest inside
    them.

There is no stoppage, and never can be stoppage;
If I and you and the worlds and all beneath or upon their
surfaces, and all the palpable life, were this moment
reduced back to a pallid float, it would not avail
in the long run;
We should surely bring up again where we now stand,
And as surely go as much farther, and then farther and
farther.

A few quadrillions of eras, a few octillions of cubic leagues,
do not hazard the span, or make it impatient,
They are but parts.... any thing is but a part.

See ever so far.... there is limitless space outside of that,
Count ever so much.... there is limitless time around that.

Our rendezvous is fitly appointed.... God will be there
and wait till we come.

[46]
I know I have the best of time and space—and that I was
never measured, and never will be measured.

I tramp a perpetual journey,
My signs are a rain-proof coat and good shoes and a staff
cut from the woods;
No friend of mine takes his ease in my chair,
I have no chair, nor church nor philosophy;
I lead no man to a dinner-table or library or exchange,
But each man and each woman of you I lead upon a knoll,
My left hand hooks you round the waist,
My right hand points to landscapes of continents, and
a plain public road.

Not I, not any one else can travel that road for you,
You must travel it for yourself.

It is not far .... it is within reach,
Perhaps you have been on it since you were born, and
    did not know,
Perhaps it is every where on water and on land.

Shoulder your duds, and I will mine, and let us hasten forth;
Wonderful cities and free nations we shall fetch as we go.

If you tire, give me both burdens, and rest the chuff
    of your hand on my hip,
And in due time you shall repay the same service to me;
For after we start we never lie by again.

This day before dawn I ascended a hill and looked at the
    crowded heaven,
And I said to my spirit, When we become the enfolders of
    those orbs and the pleasure and knowledge of every
    thing in them, shall we be filled and satisfied then?
And my spirit said No, we level that lift to pass and
    continue beyond.

You are also asking me questions, and I hear you;
I answer that I cannot answer .... you must find out for
    yourself.

Sit awhile wayfarer,
Here are biscuits to eat and here is milk to drink,
But as soon as you sleep and renew yourself in sweet
    clothes I will certainly kiss you with my goodbye kiss
    and open the gate for your egress hence.

Long enough have you dreamed contemptible dreams,
Now I wash the gum from your eyes,
You must habit yourself to the dazzle of the light and of
    every moment of your life.

Long have you timidly waded, holding a plank by the shore,
Now I will you to be a bold swimmer,
To jump off in the midst of the sea, and rise again and nod
  to me and shout, and laughingly dash with your hair.

  [47]
I am the teacher of athletes,
He that by me spreads a wider breast than my own proves
  the width of my own,
He most honors my style who learns under it to destroy
  the teacher.

The boy I love, the same becomes a man not through
  derived power but in his own right,
Wicked, rather than virtuous out of conformity or fear,
Fond of his sweetheart, relishing well his steak,
Unrequited love or a slight cutting him worse than a
  wound cuts,
First rate to ride, to fight, to hit the bull's eyes, to sail a skiff,
  to sing a song or play on the banjo,
Preferring scars and faces pitted with smallpox over all
  latherers and those that keep out of the sun.

I teach straying from me, yet who can stray from me?
I follow you whoever you are from the present hour;
My words itch at your ears till you understand them.

I do not say these things for a dollar, or to fill up the time
  while I wait for a boat;
It is you talking just as much as myself . . . . I act as the
  tongue of you,
It was tied in your mouth . . . . in mine it begins to
  be loosened.

I swear I will never mention love or death inside a house,
And I swear I never will translate myself at all, only to
    him or her who privately stays with me in the open air.

If you would understand me go to the heights or
    water-shore,
The nearest gnat is an explanation and a drop or the
    motion of waves a key,
The maul the oar and the handsaw second my words.

No shuttered room or school can commune with me,
But roughs and little children better than they.

The young mechanic is closest to me . . . . he knows
    me pretty well,
The woodman that takes his axe and jug with him shall
    take me with him all day,
The farmboy ploughing in the field feels good at the
    sound of my voice,
In vessels that sail my words must sail . . . . I go with
    fishermen and seamen, and love them,
My face rubs to the hunter's face when he lies down alone
    in his blanket,
The driver thinking of me does not mind the jolt of
    his wagon,
The young mother and old mother shall comprehend me,
The girl and the wife rest the needle a moment and
    forget where they are,
They and all would resume what I have told them.

   [48]
I have said that the soul is not more than the body,
And I have said that the body is not more than the soul,
And nothing, not God, is greater to one than one's-self is,
And whoever walks a furlong without sympathy walks
    to his own funeral, dressed in his shroud,

And I or you pocketless of a dime may purchase the
    pick of the earth,
And to glance with an eye or show a bean in its pod
    confounds the learning of all times,
And there is no trade or employment but the young man
    following it may become a hero,
And there is no object so soft but it makes a hub for
    the wheeled universe,
And any man or woman shall stand cool and supercilious
    before a million universes.

And I call to mankind, Be not curious about God,
For I who am curious about each am not curious about God,
No array of terms can say how much I am at peace
    about God and about death.

I hear and behold God in every object, yet I understand
    God not in the least,
Nor do I understand who there can be more wonderful
    than myself.

Why should I wish to see God better than this day?
I see something of God each hour of the twenty-four, and
    each moment then,
In the faces of men and women I see God, and in my
    own face in the glass;
I find letters from God dropped in the street, and every one
    is signed by God's name,
And I leave them where they are, for I know that others
    will punctually come forever and ever.

[49]
And as to you death, and you bitter hug of mortality . . . .
    it is idle to try to alarm me.

To his work without flinching the accoucheur comes,
I see the elderhand pressing receiving supporting,
I recline by the sills of the exquisite flexible doors . . . . and
    mark the outlet, and mark the relief and escape.

And as to you corpse I think you are good manure, but that
    does not offend me,
I smell the white roses sweetscented and growing,
I reach to the leafy lips . . . . I reach to the polished breasts
    of melons.

And as to you life, I reckon you are the leavings of many
    deaths,
No doubt I have died myself ten thousand times before.

I hear you whispering there O stars of heaven,
O suns . . . . O grass of graves . . . . O perpetual transfers
    and promotions . . . . if you do not say anything
    how can I say anything?

Of the turbid pool that lies in the autumn forest,
Of the moon that descends the steeps of the soughing
    twilight,
Toss, sparkles of day and dusk . . . . toss on the black stems
    that decay in the muck,
Toss to the moaning gibberish of the dry limbs.

I ascend from the moon . . . . I ascend from the night,
And perceive of the ghastly glitter the sunbeams reflected,
And debouch to the steady and central from the offspring
    great or small.

[50]
There is that in me . . . . I do not know what it is . . . . but
    I know it is in me.

Wrenched and sweaty . . . . calm and cool then my body
    becomes;
I sleep . . . . I sleep long.

I do not know it . . . . it is without name . . . . it is a word
    unsaid,
It is not in any dictionary or utterance or symbol.

Something it swings on more than the earth I swing on,
To it the creation is the friend whose embracing awakes me.

Perhaps I might tell more . . . . Outlines! I plead for my
    brothers and sisters.

Do you see O my brothers and sisters?
It is not chaos or death . . . . it is form and union and plan
    . . . . it is eternal life . . . . it is happiness.

[51]
The past and present wilt . . . . I have filled them and emptied
    them,
And proceed to fill my next fold of the future.

Listener up there! Here you . . . . what have you to confide
    to me?
Look in my face while I snuff the sidle of evening.
Talk honestly, for no one else hears you, and I stay only
    a minute longer.

Do I contradict myself?
Very well then . . . . I contradict myself;
I am large . . . . I contain multitudes.

I concentrate toward them that are nigh .... I wait on the
    door-slab.
Who has done his day's work and will soonest be through
    with his supper?
Who wishes to walk with me?

Will you speak before I am gone? Will you prove already
    too late?

[52]
The spotted hawk swoops by and accuses me .... he
    complains of my gab and my loitering.

I too am not a bit tamed .... I too am untranslatable,
I sound my barbaric yawp over the roofs of the world.

The last scud of day holds back for me,
It flings my likeness after the rest and true as any on the
    shadowed wilds,
It coaxes me to the vapor and the dusk.

I depart as air .... I shake my white locks at the runaway
    sun,
I effuse my flesh in eddies and drift it in lacy jags.

I bequeath myself to the dirt to grow from the grass I love,
If you want me again look for me under your bootsoles.

You will hardly know who I am or what I mean,
But I shall be good health to you nevertheless,
And filter and fibre your blood.

Failing to fetch me at first keep encouraged,
Missing me one place search another,
I stop some where waiting for you.

[1855]

[A SONG FOR OCCUPATIONS]

[1]
Come closer to me,
Push close my lovers and take the best I possess,
Yield closer and closer and give me the best you possess.

This is unfinished business with me .... how is it with you?
I was chilled with the cold types and cylinder and wet paper
    between us.

I pass so poorly with paper and types .... I must pass
    with the contact of bodies and souls.

I do not thank you for liking me as I am, and liking the
    touch of me .... I know that it is good for you to do so.

Were all educations practical and ornamental well
    displayed out of me, what would it amount to?
Were I as the head teacher or charitable proprietor or wise
    statesman, what would it amount to?
Were I to you as the boss employing and paying you,
    would that satisfy you?

The learned and virtuous and benevolent, and the usual
    terms;
A man like me, and never the usual terms.

Neither a servant nor a master am I,
I take no sooner a large price than a small price .... I will
    have my own whoever enjoys me,
I will be even with you, and you shall be even with me.

If you are a workman or workwoman I stand as nigh as
the nighest that works in the same shop,
If you bestow gifts on your brother or dearest friend,
I demand as good as your brother or dearest friend,
If your lover or husband or wife is welcome by day or
night, I must be personally as welcome;
If you have become degraded or ill, then I will become
so for your sake;
If you remember your foolish and outlawed deeds, do you
think I cannot remember my foolish and outlawed
deeds?
If you carouse at the table I say I will carouse at the
opposite side of the table;
If you meet some stranger in the street and love him or
her, do I not often meet strangers in the street and
love them?
If you see a good deal remarkable in me I see just as much
remarkable in you.

Why what have you thought of yourself?
Is it you then that thought yourself less?
Is it you that thought the President greater than you? or the
rich better off then you? or the educated wiser than
you?

Because you are greasy or pimpled—or that you was once
drunk, or a thief, or diseased, or rheumatic, or a
prostitute—or are so now—or from frivolity or
impotence—or that you are no scholar, and never
saw your name in print . . . . do you give in that you
are any less immortal?

[2]
Souls of men and women! it is not you I call unseen,
unheard, untouchable and untouching;

It is not you I go argue pro and con about, and to settle
    whether you are alive or no;
I own publicly who you are, if nobody else owns . . . . and
    see and hear you, and what you give and take;
What is there you cannot give and take?

I see not merely that you are polite or whitefaced . . . .
    married or single . . . . citizens of old states or citizens
    of new states . . . . eminent in some profession . . . . a
    lady or gentleman in a parlor . . . . or dressed in the
    jail uniform . . . . or pulpit uniform,
Not only the free Utahan, Kansian, or Arkansian . . . . not
    only the free Cuban . . . . not merely the slave . . . .
    not Mexican native, or Flatfoot, or negro from Africa,
Iroquois eating the warflesh—fisheater in his lair of
    rocks and sand . . . . Esquimaux in the dark cold
    snowhouse . . . . Chinese with his transverse eyes . . . .
    Bedowee—or wandering nomad—or tabounschik
    at the head of his droves,
Grown, half-grown, and babe—of this country and every
    country, indoors and outdoors I see . . . . and all else
    is behind or through them.

The wife—and she is not one jot less than the husband,
The daughter—and she is just as good as the son,
The mother—and she is every bit as much as the father.

Offspring of those not rich—boys apprenticed to trades,
Young fellows working on farms and old fellows working
    on farms;
The naive . . . . the simple and hardy . . . . he going to the
    polls to vote . . . . he who has a good time, and he
    who has a bad time;
Mechanics, southerners, new arrivals, sailors, mano'warsmen,
    merchantmen, coasters,
All these I see . . . . but nigher and farther the same I see;

None shall escape me, and none shall wish to escape me.

I bring what you much need, yet always have,
I bring not money or amours or dress or eating....but
    I bring as good;
And send no agent or medium....and offer no
    representative of value—but offer the value itself.

There is something that comes home to one now and
    perpetually.
It is not what is printed or preached or discussed....it
    eludes discussion and print,
It is not to be put in a book....it is not in this book,
It is for you whoever you are....it is no farther from you
    than your hearing and sight are from you,
It is hinted by nearest and commonest and readiest....
    it is not them, though it is endlessly provoked by
    them....What is there ready and near you now?

You may read in many languages and read nothing about it;
You may read the President's message and read nothing
    about it there;
Nothing in the reports from the state department or
    treasury department....or in the daily papers, or
    the weekly papers,
Or in the census returns or assessors' returns or prices
    current or any accounts of stock.

    [3]
The sun and stars that float in the open air....the
    appleshaped earth and we upon it....surely the
    drift of them is something grand;
I do not know what it is except that it is grand, and that it is
    happiness,
And that the enclosing purport of us here is not a
    speculation, or bon-mot or reconnoissance,

And that it is not something which by luck may turn out
     well for us, and without luck must be a failure for us,
And not something which may yet be retracted in a certain
     contingency.

The light and shade—the curious sense of body and
     identity—the greed that with perfect complaisance
     devours all things—the endless pride and outstretching
     of man—unspeakable joys and sorrows,
The wonder every one sees in every one else he sees . . . .
     and the wonders that fill each minute of time forever
     and each acre of surface and space forever,
Have you reckoned them as mainly for a trade or
     farmwork? or for the profits of a store? or to achieve
     yourself a position? or to fill a gentleman's leisure
     or a lady's leisure?

Have you reckoned the landscape took substance and
     form that it might be painted in a picture?
Or men and women that they might be written of,
     and songs sung?
Or the attraction of gravity and the great laws and
     harmonious combinations and the fluids of the air
     as subjects for the savans?
Or the brown land and the blue sea for maps and charts?
Or the stars to be put in constellations and named fancy
     names?
Or that the growth of seeds is for agricultural tables
     or agriculture itself?

Old institutions . . . . these arts libraries legends collections
     —and the practice handed along in manufactures
     . . . . will we rate them so high?
Will we rate our prudence and business so high? . . . .
     I have no objection,

I rate them as high as the highest . . . . but a child born of a
    woman and man I rate beyond all rate.

We thought our Union grand and our Constitution grand;
I do not say they are not grand and good—for they are,
I am this day just as much in love with them as you,
But I am eternally in love with you and with all my fellows
    upon the earth.

We consider the bibles and religions divine . . . . I do not
    say they are not divine,
I say they have all grown out of you and may grow
    out of you still,
It is not they who give the life . . . . it is you who give the life;
Leaves are not more shed from the trees or trees from
    the earth than they are shed out of you.

[4]

The sum of all known value and respect I add up in
    you whoever you are;
The President is up there in the White House for you . . . .
    it is not you who are here for him,
The Secretaries act in their bureaus for you . . . . not you
    here for them,
The Congress convenes every December for you,
Laws, courts, the forming of states, the charters of cities,
    the going and coming of commerce and mails are
    all for you.

All doctrines, all politics and civilization exurge from you,
All sculpture and monuments and anything inscribed
    anywhere are tallied in you,
The gist of histories and statistics as far back as the
    records reach is in you this hour—and myths and
    tales the same;

If you were not breathing and walking here where
     would they all be?
The most renowned poems would be ashes.... orations
     and plays would be vacuums.

All architecture is what you do to it when you look upon it;
Did you think it was in the white or gray stone? or the
     lines of the arches and cornices?

All music is what awakens from you when you are
     reminded by the instruments,
It is not the violins and the cornets.... it is not the oboe
     nor the beating drums—nor the notes of the baritone
     singer singing his sweet romanza.... nor those of
     the men's chorus, nor those of the women's chorus,
It is nearer and farther than they.

[5]
Will the whole come back then?
Can each see the signs of the best by a look in the
     lookingglass? Is there nothing greater or more?
Does all sit there with you and here with me?

The old forever new things.... you foolish child!....
     the closest simplest things—this moment with you,
Your person and every particle that relates to your
     person,
The pulses of your brain waiting their chance and
     encouragement at every deed or sight;
Anything you do in public by day, and anything you do
     in secret betweendays,
What is called right and what is called wrong....
     what you behold or touch.... what causes your
     anger or wonder,
The anklechain of the slave, the bed of the bedhouse,
     the cards of the gambler, the plates of the forger;

What is seen or learned in the street, or intuitively learned,
What is learned in the public school—spelling, reading,
    writing and ciphering . . . . the blackboard and the
    teacher's diagrams:
The panes of the windows and all that appears through
    them . . . . the going forth in the morning and the aimless
    spending of the day;
(What is it that you made money? what is it that you
    got what you wanted?)
The usual routine . . . . the workshop, factory, yard,
    office, store, or desk;
The jaunt of hunting or fishing, or the life of hunting or
    fishing,
Pasturelife, foddering, milking and herding, and all
    the personnel and usages;
The plum-orchard and apple-orchard . . . . gardening . . . .
    seedlings, cuttings, flowers and vines,
Grains and manures . . marl, clay, loam . . the subsoil
    plough . . the shovel and pick and rake and hoe . .
    irrigation and draining;
The currycomb . . the horse-cloth . . the halter and
    bridle and bits . . the very wisps of straw,
The barn and barn-yard . . the bins and mangers . .
    the mows and racks:
Manufacturers . . commerce . . engineering . . the building
    of cities, and every trade carried on there . . . and the
    implements of every trade,
The anvil and tongs and hammer . . the axe and wedge . . the
    square and mitre and jointer and smoothingplane;
The plumbob and trowel and level . . the wall-scaffold, and
    the work of walls and ceilings . . or any mason-work:
The ship's compass . . the sailor's tarpaulin . . the stays
    and lanyards, and the ground-tackle for anchoring or
    mooring.

The sloop's tiller .. the pilot's wheel and bell .. the
    yatch or fishsmack .. the great gay-pennanted
    three-hundred-foot steamboat under full headway,
    with her proud fat breasts and her delicate
    swift-flashing paddles,
The trail and line and hooks and sinkers .. the seine, and
    hauling the seine;
Smallarms and rifles .... the powder and shot and caps and
    wadding .... the ordnance for war .... the carriages:
Everyday objects .... the housechairs, the carpet, the
    bed and the counterpane of the bed, and him or her
    sleeping at night, and the wind blowing, and the
    indefinite noises:
The snowstorm or rainstorm .... the two-trowsers ....
    the lodgehut in the woods, and the still-hunt:
City and country .. fireplace and candle .. gaslight and
    heater and aqueduct;
The message of the governor, mayor, or chief of police ....
    the dishes of breakfast or dinner or supper;
The bunkroom, the fire-engine, the string-team, and the
    car or truck behind;
The paper I write on or you write on .. and every word
    we write .. and every cross and twirl of the pen .. and
    the curious way we write what we think .... yet
    very faintly;
The directory, the detector, the ledger .... the books
    in ranks or the bookshelves .... the clock attached
    to the wall,
The ring on your finger .. the lady's wristlet .. the
    hammers of stonebreakers or coppersmiths .. the
    druggist's vials and jars;
The etui of surgical instruments, and the etui of oculist's
    or aurist's instruments, or dentist's instruments;
Glassblowing, grinding of wheat and corn .. casting, and
    what is cast .. tinroofing, shingledressing,

Shipcarpentering, flagging of sidewalks by flaggers . .
    dockbuilding, fishcuring, ferrying;
The pump, the piledriver, the great derrick . . the coalkiln
    and brickkiln,
Ironworks or whiteleadworks . . the sugarhouse . .
    steam-saws, and the great mills and factories;
The cottonbale . . the stevedore's hook . . the saw and
    buck of the sawyer . . the screen of the coalscreener
    . . the mould of the moulder . . the workingknife of
    the butcher;
The cylinder press . . the handpress . . the frisket and
    tympan . . the compositor's stick and rule,
The implements for daguerreotyping . . . . the tools of the
    rigger or grappler or sailmaker or blockmaker,
Goods of guttapercha or papiermache . . . . colors and
    brushes . . . . glaziers' implements,
The veneer and gluepot . . the confectioner's ornaments . .
    the decanter and glasses . . the shears and flatiron;
The awl and kneestrap . . the pint measure and quart
    measure . . the counter and stool . . the writingpen of
    quill or metal;
Billiards and tenpins . . . . the ladders and hanging ropes
    of the gymnasium, and the manly exercises;
The designs for wallpapers or oilcloths or carpets . . . . the
    fancies for goods for women . . . . the bookbinder's
    stamps;
Leatherdressing, coachmaking, boilermaking, ropetwisting,
    distilling, signpainting, limeburning, coopering,
    cottonpicking,
The walkingbeam of the steam-engine . . the throttle and
    governors, and the up and down rods,
Stavemachines and planingmachines . . . . the cart of the
    carman . . the omnibus . . the ponderous dray;
The snowplough and two engines pushing it . . . . the
    ride in the express train of only one car . . . . the swift
    go through a howling storm:

The bearhunt or coonhunt.... the bonfire of shavings in the
    open lot in the city.. the crowd of children watching;
The blows of the fighting-man.. the upper cut and
    one-two-three;
The shopwindows.... the coffins in the sexton's wareroom
    .... the fruit on the fruitstand.... the beef on the
    butcher's stall,
The bread and cakes in the bakery.... the white and red
    pork in the pork-store;
The milliner's ribbons.. the dressmaker's patterns....
    the tea-table.. the homemade sweetmeats:
The column of wants in the one-cent paper.. the news by
    telegraph.... the amusements and operas and shows:
The cotton and woolen and linen you wear.... the money
    you make and spend;
Your room and bedroom.... your piano-forte....
    the stove and cookpans,
The house you live in.... the rent.... the other tenants
    .... the deposit in the savings-bank.... the trade
    at the grocery,
The pay on Saturday night.... the going home, and
    the purchases;
In them the heft of the heaviest.... in them far more than
    you estimated, and far less also,
In them, not yourself.... you and your soul enclose all
    things, regardless of estimation,
In them your themes and hints and provokers.. if not,
    the whole earth has no themes or hints or provokers,
    and never had.

I do not affirm what you see beyond is futile.... I do
    not advise you to stop,
I do not say leadings you thought great are not great,
But I say that none lead to greater or sadder or happier
    than those lead to.

[6]

Will you seek afar off? You surely come back at last,
In things best known to you finding the best or as good
    as the best,
In folks nearest to you finding also the sweetest and
    strongest and lovingest,
Happiness not in another place, but this place . . not for
    another hour, but this hour,
Man in the first you see or touch . . . . always in your
    friend or brother or nighest neighbor . . . . Woman in
    your mother or lover or wife,
And all else thus far known giving place to men and women.

When the psalm sings instead of the singer,
When the script preaches instead of the preacher,
When the pulpit descends and goes instead of the carver
    that carved the supporting desk,
When the sacred vessels or the bits of the eucharist, or
    the lath and plast, procreate as effectually as the young
    silversmiths or bakers, or the masons in their overalls,
When a university course convinces like a slumbering
    woman and child convince,
When the minted gold in the vault smiles like the
    nightwatchman's daughter,
When warrantee deeds loafe in chairs opposite and
    are my friendly companions,
I intend to reach them my hand and make as much of them
    as I do of men and women.

[1855]

[TO THINK OF TIME]

[1]

To think of time . . . . to think through the retrospection,
To think of today . . and the ages continued henceforward.

Have you guessed you yourself would not continue? Have
      you dreaded those earth-beetles?
Have you feared the future would be nothing to you?

Is today nothing? Is the beginningless past nothing?
If the future is nothing they are just as surely nothing.

To think that the sun rose in the east . . . . that men and
      women were flexible and real and alive . . . . that
      every thing was real and alive;
To think that you and I did not see feel think nor
      bear our part,
To think that we are now here and bear our part.

[2]

Not a day passes . . not a minute or second without an
      accouchement;
Not a day passes . . not a minute or second without a corpse.

When the dull nights are over, and the dull days also,
When the soreness of lying so much in bed is over,
When the physician, after long putting off, gives the
      silent and terrible look for an answer,
When the children come hurried and weeping, and the
      brothers and sisters have been sent for,
When medicines stand unused on the shelf, and the
      camphor-smell has pervaded the rooms,

When the faithful hand of the living does not desert the
hand of the dying,
When the twitching lips press lightly on the forehead
of the dying.
When the breath ceases and the pulse of the heart ceases,
Then the corpse-limbs stretch on the bed, and the living
look upon them,
They are palpable as the living are palpable.

The living look upon the corpse with their eyesight,
But without eyesight lingers a different living and
looks curiously on the corpse.

[3]
To think that the rivers will come to flow, and the snow fall,
and fruits ripen . . and act upon others as upon us
now . . . . yet not act upon us;
To think of all these wonders of city and country . . and
others taking great interest in them . . and we taking
small interest in them.

To think how eager we are in building our houses,
To think others shall be just as eager . . and we quite
indifferent.

I see one building the house that serves him a few years
. . . . or seventy or eighty years at most;
I see one building the house that serves him longer than that.

Slowmoving and black lines creep over the whole earth
. . . . they never cease . . . . they are the burial lines,
He that was President was buried, and he that is now
President shall surely be buried.

[4]
Cold dash of waves at the ferrywharf,
Posh and ice in the river .... half-frozen mud in the streets,
A gray discouraged sky overhead .... the short last
    daylight of December,
A hearse and stages .... other vehicles give place,
The funeral of an old stagedriver .... the cortege mostly drivers.

Rapid the trot to the cemetery,
Duly rattles the deathbell .... the gate is passed .... the
    grave is halted at .... the living alight ....
    the hearse uncloses,
The coffin is lowered and settled .... the whip is laid on
    the coffin,
The earth is swiftly shovelled in .... a minute .. no one
    moves or speaks .... it is done,
He is decently put away .... is there anything more?

He was a goodfellow,
Freemouthed, quicktempered, not badlooking, able to take
    his own part,
Witty, sensitive to a slight, ready with life or death for
    a friend,
Fond of women, .. played some .. eat hearty and drank
    hearty,
Had known what it was to be flush .. grew lowspirited
    toward the last .. sickened .. was helped by a
    contribution,
Died aged forty-one years .. and that was his funeral.

Thumb extended or finger uplifted,
Apron, cape, gloves, strap .... wetweather clothes ....
    whip carefully chosen .... boss, spotter, starter,
    and hostler,
Somebody loafing on you, or you loafing on somebody ....
    headway .... man before and man behind,

Good day's work or bad day's work .... pet stock or mean
     stock .... first out or last out .... turning in at night,
To think that these are so much and so nigh to other
     drivers .... and he there takes no interest in them.

[5]

The markets, the government, the workingman's wages
     .... to think what account they are through our
     nights and days;
To think that other workingmen will make just as great
     account of them .. yet we make little or no account.

The vulgar and the refined .... what you call sin and
     what you call goodness .. to think how wide a
     difference;
To think the difference will still continue to others,
     yet we lie beyond the difference.

To think how much pleasure there is!
Have you pleasure from looking at the sky? Have you
     pleasure from poems?
Do you enjoy yourself in the city? or engaged in business?
     or planning a nomination and election? or with your
     wife and family?
Or with your mother and sisters? or in womanly housework?
     or the beautiful maternal cares?

These also flow onward to others .... you and I flow onward;
But in due time you and I shall take less interest in them.

Your farm and profits and crops .... to think how
     engrossed you are;
To think there will still be farms and profits and crops
     .. yet for you of what avail?

[6]
What will be will be well—for what is is well,
To take interest is well, and not to take interest shall be
  well.

The sky continues beautiful.... the pleasure of men with
  women shall never be sated.. nor the pleasure of
  women with men.. nor the pleasure from poems;
The domestic joys, the daily housework or business, the
  building of houses—they are not phantasms.. they
  have weight and form and location;
The farms and profits and crops.. the markets and wages
  and government.. they also are not phantasms;
The difference between sin and goodness is no apparition;
The earth is not an echo.... man and his life and all the
  things of his life are well-considered.

You are not thrown to the winds.. you gather certainly
  and safely around yourself,
Yourself! Yourself! Yourself forever and ever!

[7]
It is not to diffuse you that you were born of your mother
  and father—it is to identify you,
It is not that you should be undecided, but that you
  should be decided;
Something long preparing and formless is arrived and
  formed in you,
You are thenceforth secure, whatever comes or goes.

The threads that were spun are gathered.... the weft
  crosses the warp.... the pattern is systematic.

The preparations have every one been justified;
The orchestra have tuned their instruments sufficiently....
  the baton has given the signal.

The guest that was coming .... he waited long for reasons
    .... he is now housed,
He is one of those who are beautiful and happy .... he is
    one of those that to look upon and be with is enough.
The law of the past cannot be eluded,
The law of the present and future cannot be eluded,
The law of the living cannot be eluded .... it is eternal,
The law of promotion and transformation cannot be eluded,
The law of heroes and good-doers cannot be eluded,
The law of drunkards and informers and mean persons
    cannot be eluded.

[8]

Slowmoving and black lines go ceaselessly over the earth,
Northerner goes carried and southerner goes carried ...
    and they on the Atlantic side and they on the
    Pacific, and they between, and all through the
    Mississippi country .... and all over the earth.

The great masters and kosmos are well as they go .... the
    heroes and good-doers are well,
The known leaders and inventors and the rich owners
    and pious and distinguished may be well,
But there is more account than that .... there is strict
    account of all.

The interminable hordes of the ignorant and wicked are
    not nothing.
The barbarians of Africa and Asia are not nothing.
The common people of Europe are not nothing .... the
    American aborigines are not nothing.
A zambo or a foreheadless Crowfoot or a Camanche is not
    nothing,
The infected in the immigrant hospital are not nothing
    .... the murderer or mean person is not nothing.
The perpetual succession of shallow people are not
    nothing as they go,

The prostitute is not nothing . . . . the mocker of religion
    is not nothing as he goes.

I shall go with the rest . . . . we have satisfaction:
I have dreamed that we are not to be changed so much
    . . . . nor the law of us changed;
I have dreamed that heroes and good-doers shall be under
    the present and past law,
And that murderers and drunkards and liars shall be
    under the present and past law;
For I have dreamed that the law they are under now
    is enough.

And I have dreamed that the satisfaction is not so much
    changed . . . . and that there is no life without
    satisfaction;
What is the earth? what are body and soul without
    satisfaction?

I shall go with the rest,
We cannot be stopped at a given point . . . . that is no
    satisfaction;
To show us a good thing or a few good things for a space of
    time—that is no satisfaction;
We must have the indestructible breed of the best,
    regardless of time.

If otherwise, all these things came but to ashes of dung;
If maggots and rats ended us, then suspicion and treachery
    and death.

Do you suspect death? If I were to suspect death I should
    die now,
Do you think I could walk pleasantly and well-suited
    toward annihilation?

Pleasantly and well-suited I walk,
Whither I walk I cannot define, but I know it is good,
The whole universe indicates that it is good,
The past and the present indicate that it is good.

How beautiful and perfect are the animals! How perfect
    is my soul!
How perfect the earth, and the minutest thing upon it!
What is called good is perfect, and what is called
    sin is just as perfect;
The vegetables and minerals are perfect.. and the
    imponderable fluids are perfect;
Slowly and surely they have passed on to this, and slowly
    and surely they will yet pass on.

O my soul! if I realize you I have satisfaction,
Animals and vegetables! if I realize you I have satisfaction,
Laws of the earth and air! if I realize you I have
    satisfaction.
I cannot define my satisfaction.. yet it is so,
I cannot define my life.. yet it is so.

[9]
I swear I see now that every thing has an eternal soul!
The trees have, rooted in the ground .... the weeds of
    the sea have .... the animals.

I swear I think there is nothing but immortality!
That the exquisite scheme is for it, and the nebulous
    float is for it, and the cohering is for it,
And all preparing is for it.. and identity is for it..
    and life and death are for it.

[1855]

[THE SLEEPERS]

[1]

I wander all night in my vision,
Stepping with light feet.... swiftly and noiselessly stepping
    and stopping,
Bending with open eyes over the shut eyes of sleepers;
Wandering and confused.... lost to myself.... ill-assorted
    .... contradictory,
Pausing and gazing and bending and stopping.

How solemn they look there, stretched and still;
How quiet they breathe, the little children in their cradles.

The wretched features of ennuyees, the white features
    of corpses, the livid faces of drunkards, the sick-gray
    faces of onanists,
The gashed bodies on battlefields, the insane in their
    strong-doored rooms, the sacred idiots,
The newborn emerging from gates and the dying
    emerging from gates,
The night pervades them and enfolds them.

The married couple sleep calmly in their bed, he with
    his palm on the hip of the wife, and she with her
    palm on the hip of the husband,
The sisters sleep lovingly side by side in their bed,
The men sleep lovingly side by side in theirs,
And the mother sleeps with her little child carefully
    wrapped.

The blind sleep, and the deaf and dumb sleep,
The prisoner sleeps well in the prison.... the runaway
    son sleeps,

The murderer that is to be hung next day . . . .
    how does he sleep?
And the murdered person . . . . how does he sleep?

The female that loves unrequited sleeps,
And the male that loves unrequited sleeps;
The head of the moneymaker that plotted all day sleeps,
And the enraged and treacherous dispositions sleep.

I stand with drooping eyes by the worstsuffering and restless,
I pass my hands soothingly to and fro a few inches from
    them;
The restless sink in their beds . . . . they fitfully sleep.

The earth recedes from me into the night,
I saw that it was beautiful . . . . and I see that what is not
    the earth is beautiful.

I go from bedside to bedside . . . . I sleep close with
    the other sleepers, each in turn;
I dream in my dream all the dreams of the other dreamers,
And I become the other dreamers.

I am a dance . . . . Play up there! the fit is whirling me fast.

I am the everlaughing . . . . it is new moon and twilight,
I see the hiding of douceurs . . . . I see nimble ghosts
    whichever way I look,
Cache and cache again deep in the ground and sea, and
    where it is neither ground or sea.

Well do they do their jobs, those journeymen divine,
Only from me can they hide nothing and would not
    if they could;
I reckon I am their boss, and they make me a pet besides,
And surround me, and lead me and run ahead when I walk,

And lift their cunning covers and signify me with
    stretched arms, and resume the way;
Onward we move, a gay gang of blackguards with
    mirthshouting music and wildflapping pennants of joy.

I am the actor and the actress . . . . the voter . . the politician,
The emigrant and the exile . . the criminal that stood
    in the box,
He who has been famous, and he who shall be famous
    after today,
The stammerer . . . . the wellformed person . . the wasted or
    feeble person.

I am she who adorned herself and folded her hair
    expectantly,
My truant lover has come and it is dark.

Double yourself and receive me darkness,
Receive me and my lover too . . . . he will not let me go
    without him.

I roll myself upon you as upon a bed . . . . I resign myself
    to the dusk.

He whom I call answers me and takes the place of my lover,
He rises with me silently from the bed.

Darkness you are gentler than my lover . . . . his flesh was
    sweaty and panting.
I feel the hot moisture yet that he left me.

My hands are spread forth . . I pass them in all directions,
I would sound up the shadowy shore to which you are
    journeying.

Be careful, darkness . . . . already, what was it touched me?

I thought my lover had gone . . . . else darkness and he are one,
I hear the heart-beat . . . . I follow . . I fade away.

O hotcheeked and blushing! O foolish hectic!
O for pity's sake, no one must see me now! . . . . my
    clothes were stolen while I was abed,
Now I am thrust forth, where shall I run?

Pier that I saw dimly last night when I looked from the
    windows,
Pier out from the main, let me catch myself with you and
    stay . . . . I will not chafe you;
I feel ashamed to go naked about the world,
And am curious to know where my feet stand . . . . and
    what is this flooding me, childhood or manhood . . . .
    and the hunger that crosses the bridge between.

The cloth laps a first sweet eating and drinking,
Laps life-swelling yolks . . . . laps ear of rose-corn, milky
    and just ripened:
The white teeth stay, and the boss-tooth advances in
    darkness,
And liquor is spilled on lips and bosoms by touching
    glasses, and the best liquor afterward.

[2]
I descend my western course . . . . my sinews are flaccid,
Perfume and youth course through me, and I am their wake.

It is my face yellow and wrinkled instead of the old
    woman's,
I sit low in a strawbottom chair and carefully darn my
    grandson's stockings.

It is I too . . . . the sleepless widow looking out on the winter
    midnight,
I see the sparkles of starshine on the icy and pallid earth.

A shroud I see—and I am the shroud . . . . I wrap a
    body and lie in the coffin;
It is dark here underground . . . . it is not evil or pain
    here . . . . it is blank here, for reasons.

It seems to me that everything in the light and air ought
    to be happy;
Whoever is not in his coffin and the dark grave, let him
    know he has enough.

[3]
I see a beautiful gigantic swimmer swimming naked through
    the eddies of the sea,
His brown hair lies close and even to his head . . . . he
    strikes out with courageous arms . . . . he urges
    himself with his legs.

I see his white body . . . . I see his undaunted eyes;
I hate the swift-running eddies that would dash him
    headforemost on the rocks.

What are you doing you ruffianly red-trickled waves?
Will you kill the courageous giant? Will you kill him
    in the prime of his middle age?

Steady and long he struggles;
He is baffled and banged and bruised . . . . he holds out
    while his strength holds out,
The slapping eddies are spotted with his blood . . . . they
    bear him away . . . . they roll him and swing him
    and turn him:
His beautiful body is borne in the circling eddies . . . .
    it is continually bruised on rocks,
Swiftly and out of sight is borne the brave corpse.

[4]

I turn but do not extricate myself;
Confused . . . . a pastreading . . . . another, but with darkness
    yet.

The beach is cut by the razory ice-wind . . . . the wreck-guns
    sounds,
The tempest lulls and the moon comes floundering
    through the drifts.

I look where the ship helplessly heads end on . . . . I hear
    the burst as she strikes . . I hear the howls of dismay
    . . . . they grow fainter and fainter.

I cannot aid with my wringing fingers;
I can but rush to the surf and let it drench me and freeze
    upon me.

I search with the crowd . . . . not one of the company is
    washed to us alive;
In the morning I help pick up the dead and lay them in
    rows in a barn.

[5]

Now of the old war-days . . the defeat at Brooklyn;
Washington stands inside the lines . . he stands on the
    entrenched hills amid a crowd of officers,
His face is cold and damp . . . . he cannot repress the weeping
    drops . . . . he lifts the glass perpetually to his eyes
    . . . . the color is blanched from his cheeks,
He sees the slaughter of the southern braves confided to
    him by their parents.

The same at last and at last when peace is declared,
He stands in the room of the old tavern . . . . the wellbeloved
    soldiers all pass through.

The officers speechless and slow draw near in their turns,
The chief encircles their necks with his arm and kisses
    them on the cheek,
He kisses lightly the wet cheeks one after another....
    he shakes hands and bids goodbye to the army.

[6]
Now I tell what my mother told me today as we sat
    at dinner together,
Of when she was a nearly grown girl living home with her
    parents on the old homestead.

A red squaw came one breakfasttime to the old homestead,
On her back she carried a bundle of rushes for
    rushbottoming chairs;
Her hair straight shiny coarse black and profuse
    halfenveloped her face,
Her step was free and elastic.... her voice sounded
    exquisitely as she spoke.

My mother looked in delight and amazement at the stranger,
She looked at the beauty of her tallborne face and full
    and pliant limbs,
The more she looked upon her she loved her,
Never before had she seen such wonderful beauty and
    purity;
She made her sit on a bench by the jamb of the fireplace
    .... she cooked food for her,
She had no work to give her but she gave her remembrance
    and fondness.

The red squaw staid all the forenoon, and toward the
    middle of the afternoon she went away;
O my mother was loth to have her go away,
All the week she thought of her.... she watched for her
    many a month,

She remembered her many a winter and many a summer,
But the red squaw never came nor was heard of there again.

Now Lucifer was not dead . . . . or if he was I am his
    sorrowful terrible heir;
I have been wronged . . . . I am oppressed . . . . I hate
    him that oppresses me,
I will either destroy him, or he shall release me.

Damn him! how he does defile me,
How he informs against my brother and sister and takes
    pay for their blood,
How he laughs when I look down the bend after the
    steamboat that carries away my woman.

Now the vast dusk bulk that is the whale's bulk . . . it seems
    mine,
Warily, sportsman! though I lie so sleepy and sluggish,
    my tap is death.

    [7]
A show of the summer softness . . . . a contract of something
    unseen . . . . an amour of the light and air;
I am jealous and overwhelmed with friendliness,
And will go gallivant with the light and the air myself,
And have an unseen something to be in contact with
    them also.

O love and summer! you are in the dreams and in me,
Autumn and winter are in the dreams . . . . the farmer
    goes with his thrift,
The droves and crops increase . . . . the barns are wellfilled.

Elements merge in the night . . . . ships make tacks in
    the dreams . . . . the sailor sails . . . . the exile
    returns home,

The fugitive returns unharmed . . . . the immigrant is back
    beyond months and years;
The poor Irishman lives in the simple house of his
    childhood, with the wellknown neighbors and faces,
They warmly welcome him . . . . he is barefoot again
    . . . . he forgets he is welloff;
The Dutchman voyages home, and the Scotchman and
    Welchman voyage home . . and the native of the
    Mediterranean voyages home;
To every port of England and France and Spain enter
    wellfilled ships;
The Swiss foots it toward his hills . . . . the Prussian goes
    his way, and the Hungarian his way, and the Pole
    goes his way,
The Swede returns, and the Dane and Norwegian return.

The homeward bound and the outward bound,
The beautiful lost swimmer, the ennuyee, the onanist,
    the female that loves unrequited, the moneymaker,
The actor and actress . . those through with their parts
    and those waiting to commence,
The affectionate boy, the husband and wife, the voter,
    the nominee that is chosen and the nominee that
    has failed,
The great already known, and the great anytime after
    to day,
The stammerer, the sick, the perfectformed, the homely,
The criminal that stood in the box, the judge that sat and
    sentenced him, the fluent lawyers, the jury, the audience,
The laugher and weeper, the dancer, the midnight widow,
    the red squaw,
The consumptive, the crysipalite, the idiot, he that is
    wronged,
The antipodes, and every one between this and them
    in the dark,

I swear they are averaged now .... one is no better than
    the other,
The night and sleep have likened them and restored them.

I swear they are all beautiful,
Every one that sleeps is beautiful .... every thing in the
    dim night is beautiful,
The wildest and bloodiest is over and all is peace.

Peace is always beautiful,
The myth of heaven indicates peace and night.

The myth of heaven indicates the soul;
The soul is always beautiful .... it appears more or it
    appears less .... it comes or lags behind,
It comes from its embowered garden and looks pleasantly
    on itself and encloses the world;
Perfect and clean the genitals previously jetting, and perfect
    and clean the womb cohering,
The head wellgrown and proportioned and plumb, and
    the bowels and joints proportioned and plumb.

The soul is always beautiful,
The universe is duly in order .... every thing is in its place,
What is arrived is in its place, and what waits is in
    its place;
The twisted skull waits .... the watery or rotten blood
    waits,
The child of the glutton or venerealee waits long, and the
    child of the drunkard waits long, and the drunkard
    himself waits long.
The sleepers that lived and died wait .... the far advanced
    are to go on in their turns, and the far behind are
    to go on in their turns,
The diverse shall be no less diverse, but they shall flow
    and unite .... they unite now.

[8]
The sleepers are very beautiful as they lie unclothed,
They flow hand in hand over the whole earth from east to
        west as they lie unclothed;
The Asiatic and African are hand in hand . . the
        European and American are hand in hand,
Learned and unlearned are hand in hand . . and male
        and female are hand in hand;
The bare arm of the girl crosses the bare breast of her
        lover . . . . they press close without lust . . . . his lips
        press her neck,
The father holds his grown or ungrown son in his arms with
        measureless love . . . . and the son holds the father
        in his arms with measureless love,
The white hair of the mother shines on the white wrist
        of the daughter,
The breath of the boy goes with the breath of the man
        . . . . friend is inarmed by friend,
The scholar kisses the teacher and the teacher kisses
        the scholar . . . . the wronged is made right,
The call of the slave is one with the master's call . . and
        the master salutes the slave,
The felon steps forth from the prison . . . . the insane
        becomes sane . . . . the suffering of sick persons
        is relieved,
The sweatings and fevers stop . . the throat that was
        unsound is sound . . the lungs of the consumptive are
        resumed . . the poor distressed head is free,
The joints of the rheumatic move as smoothly as ever,
        and smoother than ever,
Stiflings and passages open . . . . the paralysed become
        supple,
The swelled and convulsed and congested awake to
        themselves in condition,
They pass the invigoration of the night and the chemistry
        of the night and awake.

I too pass from the night;
I stay awhile away O night, but I return to you again
    and love you;
Why should I be afraid to trust myself to you?
I am not afraid . . . . I have been well brought forward by
    you;
I love the rich running day, but I do not desert her in
    whom I lay so long:
I know not how I came of you, and I know not where I go
    with you . . . . but I know I came well and shall go well.

I will stop only a time with the night . . . . and rise betimes.
I will duly pass the day O my mother and duly return to you;
Not you will yield forth the dawn again more surely
    than you will yield forth me again,
Not the womb yields the babe in its time more surely than
    I shall be yielded from you in my time.

[1855]

[I SING THE BODY ELECTRIC]

[1]

The bodies of men and women engirth me, and I engirth
    them,
They will not let me off nor I them till I go with them and
    respond to them and love them.

Was it dreamed whether those who corrupted their
    own live bodies could conceal themselves?
And whether those who defiled the living were as bad as
    they who defiled the dead?

The expression of the body of man or woman balks account,
The male is perfect and that of the female is perfect.

The expression of a wellmade man appears not only in
    his face,
It is in his limbs and joints also .... it is curiously
    in the joints of his hips and wrists,
It is in his walk .. the carriage of his neck .. the flex of
    his waist and knees .... dress does not hide him,
The strong sweet supple quality he has strikes through the
    cotton and flannel;
To see him pass conveys as much as the best poem ..
    perhaps more,
You linger to see his back and the back of his neck
    and shoulderside.

The sprawl and fulness of babes .... the bosoms and
    heads of women .... the folds of their dress ....
    their style as we pass in the street .... the contour of
    their shape downwards;
The swimmer naked in the swimmingbath .. seen as
    he swims through the salt transparent greenshine, or
    lies on his back and rolls silently with the heave
    of the water;
Framers bare-armed framing a house .. hoisting the
    beams in their places .. or using the mallet and
    mortising-chisel,
The bending forward and backward of rowers in
    rowboats .... the horseman in his saddle;
Girls and mothers and housekeepers in all their
    exquisite offices,
The group of laborers seated at noontime with their open
    dinner-kettles, and their wives waiting,

The female soothing a child .... the farmer's daughter
    in the garden or cowyard,
The woodman rapidly swinging his axe in the woods
    .... the young fellow hoeing corn .... the sleighdriver
    guiding his six horses through the crowd,
The wrestle of wrestlers .... two apprentice-boys,
    quite grown, lusty, goodnatured, nativeborn, out on
    the vacant lot at sun-down after work,
The coats vests and caps thrown down .. the embrace
    of love and resistance,
The upperhold and underhold—the hair rumpled over and
    blinding the eyes;
The march of firemen in their own costumes—the play
    of the masculine muscle through cleansetting trowsers
    and waistbands,
The slow return from the fire .... the pause when
    the bell strikes suddenly again—the listening on the alert,
The natural perfect and varied attitudes .... the bent
    head, the curved neck, the counting:
Suchlike I love .... I loosen myself and pass freely ....
    and am at the mother's breast with the little child,
And swim with the swimmer, and wrestle with
    wrestlers, and march in line with the firemen, and
    pause and listen and count.

    [3]
I knew a man .... he was a common farmer .... he was
    the father of five sons .... and in them were the fathers
    of sons .... and in them were the fathers of sons.

This man was of wonderful vigor and calmness
    and beauty of person;
The shape of his head, the richness and breadth of his
    manners, the pale yellow and white of his hair
    and beard, the immeasurable meaning of his black eyes,

These I used to go and visit him to see . . . . He was wise also,
He was six feet tall . . . . he was over eighty years old . . . .
    his sons were massive clean bearded tanfaced
    and handsome,
They and his daughters loved him . . . all who saw him
    loved him . . . they did not love him by allowance . . .
    they loved him with personal love;
He drank water only . . . . the blood showed like scarlet
    through the clear brown skin of his face;
He was a frequent gunner and fisher . . . he sailed his
    boat himself . . . he had a fine one presented to him
    by a shipjoiner . . . . he had fowling pieces, presented to
    him by men that loved him;
When he went with his five sons and many grandsons
    to hunt or fish you would pick him out as the most
    beautiful and vigorous of the gang,
You would wish long and long to be with him . . . .
    you would wish to sit by him in the boat that you and
    he might touch each other.

    [4]
I have perceived that to be with those I like is enough,
To stop in company with the rest at evening is enough,
To be surrounded by beautiful curious breathing laughing
    flesh is enough,
To pass among them . . to touch any one . . . . to rest
    my arm ever so lightly round his or her neck for a
    moment . . . . what is this then?
I do not ask any more delight . . . . I swim in it as in a sea.

There is something in staying close to men and women
    and looking on them and in the contact and odor
    of them that pleases the soul well,
All things please the soul, but these please the soul well.

[5]
This is the female form,
A divine nimbus exhales from it from head to foot,
It attracts with fierce undeniable attraction,
I am drawn by its breath as if I were no more than a helpless
    vapor . . . . all falls aside but myself and it,
Books, art, religion, time . . the visible and solid earth . .
    the atmosphere and the fringed clouds . . what was
    expected of heaven or feared of hell are now consumed,
Mad filaments, ungovernable shoots play out of it . . the
    response likewise ungovernable,
Hair, bosom, hips, bend of legs, negligent falling
    hands—all diffused . . . . mine too diffused,
Ebb stung by the flow, and flow stung by the ebb . . . .
    loveflesh swelling and deliciously aching,
Limitless limpid jets of love hot and enormous . . . .
    quivering jelly of love . . . . white-blow and delirious
    juice,
Bridegroom-night of love working surely and softly
    into the prostrate dawn,
Undulating into the willing and yielding day,
Lost in the cleave of the clasping and sweetfleshed day.

This is the nucleus . . . after the child is born of
    woman the man is born of woman,
This is the bath of birth . . . this is the merge of small and
    large and the outlet again.

Be not ashamed women . . your privilege encloses the
    rest . . it is the exit of the rest,
You are the gates of the body and you are the gates
    of the soul.

The female contains all qualities and tempers them
    . . . . she is in her place . . . . she moves with perfect
    balance,

She is all things duly veiled .... she is both passive
    and active .... she is to conceive daughters as well as
    sons and sons as well as daughters.

As I see my soul reflected in nature .... as I see through
    a mist one with inexpressible completeness and beauty
    .... see the bent head and arms folded over the
    breast .... the female I see,
I see the bearer of the great fruit which is immortality
    .... the good thereof is not tasted by roues, and
    never can be.

[6]
The male is not less the soul, nor more .... he too is
    in his place,
He too is all qualities .... he is action and power ....
    the flush of the known universe is in him,
Scorn becomes him well and appetite and defiance
    become him well,
The fiercest largest passions .. bliss that is utmost and sorrow
    that is utmost become him well .... pride is for him,
The fullspread pride of man is calming and excellent
    to the soul;
Knowledge becomes him .... he likes it always ....
    he brings everything to the test of himself,
Whatever the survey .. whatever the sea and the sail,
    he strikes soundings at last only here,
Where else does he strike soundings except here?

The man's body is sacred and the woman's body is sacred
    .... it is no matter who,
Is it a slave? Is it one of the dullfaced immigrants
    just landed on the wharf?

Each belongs here or anywhere just as much as the welloff
    .... just as much as you,
Each has his or her place in the procession.

All is a procession,
The universe is a procession with measured and beautiful motion.

Do you know so much that you call the salve or the
  dullfaced ignorant?
Do you suppose you have a right to a good sight . . . and
  he or she has no right to a sight?
Do you think matter has cohered together from its
  diffused float, and the soil is on the surface and water
  runs and vegetation sprouts for you . . and not for
  him and her?

  [7]
A slave at auction!
I help the auctioneer . . . . the sloven does not half know his
  business.

Gentlemen look on this curious creature,
Whatever the bids of the bidders they cannot be high enough
  for him,
For him the globe lay preparing quintillions of years without
  one animal or plant,
For him the revolving cycles truly and steadily rolled.

In that head the allbaffling brain,
In it and below it the making of the attributes of heroes.

Examine these limbs, red black or white . . . . they are
  very cunning in tendon and nerve;
They shall be stript that you may see them.

Exquisite senses, lifelit eyes, pluck, volition,
Flakes of breastmuscle, pliant backbone and neck, flesh
  not flabby, goodsized arms and legs,
And wonders within there yet.

Within there runs his blood . . . . the same old blood . . . .
   the same red running blood;
There swells and jets his heart . . . . There all passions and
   desires . . all reachings and aspirations:
Do you think they are not there because they are not
   expressed in parlors and lecture-rooms?

This is not only one man . . . . he is the father of those
   who shall be fathers in their turns,
In him the start of populous states and rich republics,
Of him countless immortal lives with countless embodiments
   and enjoyments.

How do you know who shall come from the offspring of
   his offspring through the centuries?
Who might you find you have come from yourself if you
   could trace back through the centuries?

   [8]
A woman at auction,
She too is not only herself . . . . she is the teeming mother
   of mothers,
She is the bearer of them that shall grow and be mates
   to the mothers.

Her daughters or their daughters' daughters . . who
   knows who shall mate with them?
Who knows through the centuries what heroes may come
   from them?

In them and of them natal love . . . . in them the divine
   mystery . . . . the same old beautiful mystery.
Have you ever loved a woman?

Your mother . . . . is she living? . . . . Have you been
    much with her? and has she been much with you?
Do you not see that these are exactly the same to all in all
    nations and times all over the earth?

If life and the soul are sacred the human body is sacred;
And the glory and sweet of a man is the token of manhood
    untainted,
And in man or woman a clean strong firmfibred body
    is beautiful as the most beautiful face.

Have you seen the fool that corrupted his own live body?
    or the fool that corrupted her own live body?
For they do not conceal themselves, and cannot conceal
    themselves.

Who degrades or defiles the living human body is cursed,
Who degrades or defiles the body of the dead is not
    more cursed.

                           [1855]

[THERE WAS A CHILD WENT FORTH]

There was a child went forth every day,
And the first object he looked upon and received with
    wonder or pity or love or dread, that object
    he became,
And that object became part of him for the day or a certain
    part of the day . . . . or for many years or stretching
    cycles of years.

The early lilacs became part of this child,
And grass, and white and red morningglories, and white
    and red clover, and the song of the phœbe-bird,
And the March-born lambs, and the sow's pink-faint litter,
    and the mare's foal, and the cow's calf, and the
    noisy brood of the barnyard or by the mire of the
    pondside . . and the fish suspending themselves so
    curiously below there . . and the beautiful curious
    liquid . . and the water-plants with their grateful flat
    heads . . all became part of him.

And the field-sprouts of April and May became part of him
    . . . . wintergrain sprouts, and those of the light-yellow
    corn, and of the esculent roots of the garden,
And the appletrees covered with blossoms, and the fruit
    afterward . . . . and woodberries . . and the commonest
    weeds by the road;
And the old drunkard staggering home from the outhouse
    of the tavern whence he had lately risen,
And the schoolmistress that passed on her way to the
    school . . and the friendly boys that passed . . and
    the quarrelsome boys . . and the tidy and freshcheeked
    girls . . and the barefoot negro boy and girl,
And all the changes of city and country wherever he went.

His own parents . . he that had propelled the fatherstuff
    at night, and fathered him . . and she that conceived
    him in her womb and birthed him . . . . they gave
    this child more of themselves than that,
They gave him afterward every day . . . . they and of them
    became part of him.

The mother at home quietly placing the dishes on the
    suppertable,
The mother with mild words . . . . clean her cap and
    gown . . . . a wholesome odor falling off her person and
    clothes as she walks by:

The father, strong, selfsufficient, manly, mean, angered,
    unjust,
The blow, the quick loud word, the tight bargain, the crafty
    lure,
The family usages, the language, the company, the
    furniture . . . . the yearning and swelling heart,
Affection that will not be gainsayed . . . . The sense of
    what is real . . . . the thought if after all it should
    prove unreal,
The doubts of daytime and the doubts of nighttime . . .
    the curious whether and how,
Whether that which appears so is so . . . . Or is it all
    flashes and specks?
Men and women crowding fast in the streets . . if they
    are not flashes and specks what are they?
The streets themselves, and the facades of houses . . . .
    the goods in the windows,
Vehicles . . teams . . the tiered wharves, and the huge
    crossing at the ferries;
The village on the highland seen from afar at sunset . . . .
    the river between,
Shadows . . aureola and mist . . light falling on roofs and
    gables of white or brown, three miles off,
The schooner near by sleepily dropping down the tide . .
    the little boat slacktowed astern,
The hurrying tumbling waves and quickbroken crests
    and slapping;
The strata of colored clouds . . . . the long bar of
    maroontint away solitary by itself . . . . the spread
    of purity it lies motionless in,
The horizon's edge, the flying seacrow, the fragrance of
    saltmarsh and shoremud;
These became part of that child who went forth every day,
    and who now goes and will always go forth every day,
And these become of him or her that peruses them now.
                                                    [1855]

SONG OF THE BROAD-AXE

1

Weapon shapely, naked, wan,
Head from the mother's bowels drawn,
Wooded flesh and metal bone, limb only one and lip
    only one,
Gray-blue leaf by red-heat grown, helve produced from
    a little seed sown,
Resting the grass amid and upon,
To be lean'd and to lean on.

Strong shapes and attributes of strong shapes, masculine
    trades, sights and sounds,
Long varied train of an emblem, dabs of music,
Fingers of the organist skipping staccato over the keys
    of the great organ.

2

Welcome are all earth's lands, each for its kind,
Welcome are lands of pine and oak,
Welcome are lands of the lemon and fig,
Welcome are lands of gold,
Welcome are lands of wheat and maize, welcome those of
    the grape,
Welcome are lands of sugar and rice,
Welcome the cotton-lands, welcome those of the white
    potato and sweet potato,
Welcome are mountains, flats, sands, forests, prairies,
Welcome the rich borders of rivers, table-lands, openings,
Welcome the measureless grazing-lands, welcome the
    teeming soil of orchards, flax, honey, hemp;
Welcome just as much the other more hard-faced lands,
Lands rich as lands of gold or wheat and fruit lands,

Lands of miens, lands of the manly and rugged ores,
Lands of coal, copper, lead, tin, zinc,
Lands of iron—lands of the make of the axe.

3

The log at the wood-pile, the axe supported by it,
The sylvan hut, the vine over the doorway, the space clear'd
    for a garden,
The irregular tapping of rain down on the leaves after the
    storm is lull'd,
The wailing and moaning at intervals, the thought of the sea,
The thought of ships struck in the storm and put on their
    beam ends, and the cutting away of masts,
The sentiment of the huge timbers of old-fashion'd
    houses and barns.
The remember'd print or narrative, the voyage at a
    venture of men, families, goods,
The disembarkation, the founding of a new city,
The voyage of those who sought a New England and
    found it, the outset anywhere,
The settlements of the Arkansas, Colorado, Ottawa,
    Willamette,
The slow progress, the scant fare, the axe, rifle, saddle-bags;
The beauty of all adventurous and daring persons,
The beauty of wood-boys and wood-men with their clear
    untrimm'd faces,
The beauty of independence, departure, actions that rely
    on themselves,
The American contempt for statutes and ceremonies,
    the boundless impatience of restraint,
The loose drift of character, the inkling through random
    types, the solidification;
The butcher in the slaughter-house, the hands aboard
    schooners and sloops, the raftsman, the pioneer,

Lumbermen in their winter camp, daybreak in the
    woods, stripes of snow on the limbs of trees,
    the occasional snapping,
The glad clear sound of one's own voice, the merry song,
    the natural life of the woods, the strong day's work,
The blazing fire at night, the sweet taste of supper, the talk,
    the bed of hemlock-boughs and the bear-skin;
The house-builder at work in cities or anywhere,
The preparatory jointing, squaring sawing, mortising,
The hoist-up of beams, the push of them in their places,
    laying them regular,
Setting the studs by their tenons in the mortises according
    as they were prepared,
The blows of mallets and hammers, the attitudes of
    the men, their curv'd limbs,
Bending, standing, astride the beams, driving in pins,
    holding on by posts and braces,
The hook'd arm over the plate, the other arm wielding
    the axe,
The floor-men forcing the planks close to be nail'd,
Their postures bringing their weapons downward on the
    bearers,
The echoes resounding through the vacant building;
The huge storehouse carried up in the city well under way,
The six framing-men, two in the middle and two at
    each end, carefully bearing on their shoulders
    a heavy stick for a cross-beam,
The crowded line of masons with trowels in their
    right hands rapidly laying the long side-wall,
    two hundred feet from front to rear,
The flexible rise and fall of backs, the continual click
    of the trowels striking the bricks,
The bricks one after another each laid so workmanlike
    in its place, and set with a knock of the trowel-handle,
The piles of materials, the mortar on the mortar-boards,
    and the steady replenishing by the hod-men;

Spar-makers in the spar-yard, the swarming row of
    well-grown apprentices,
The swing of their axes on the square-hew'd log shaping
    it toward the shape of a mast,
The brisk short crackle of the steel driven slantingly into
    the pipe,
The butter-color'd chips flying off in great flakes and slivers,
The limber motion of brawny young arms and hips
    in easy costumes,
The constructor of wharves, bridges, piers, bulk-heads,
    floats, stays against the sea;
The city fireman, the fire that suddenly bursts forth in the
    close-pack'd square,
The arriving engines, the hoarse shouts, the nimble stepping
    and daring,
The strong command through the fire-trumpets, the falling in
    line, the rise and fall of the arms forcing the water,
The slender, spasmic, blue-white jets, the bringing to
    bear of the hooks and ladders and their execution,
The crash and cut away of connecting wood-work, or
    through floors if the fire smoulders under them.
The crowd with their lit faces watching, the glare and
    dense shadows;
The forger at his forge-furnace and the user of iron after him,
The maker of the axe large and small, and the welder
    and temperer,
The chooser breathing his breath on the cold steel and trying
    the edge with his thumb,
The one who clean-shapes the handle and sets it firmly
    in the socket;
The shadowy processions of the portraits of the past
    users also,
The primal patient mechanics, the architects and engineers,
The far-off Assyrian edifice and Mizra edifice,
The Roman lictors preceding the consuls,
The antique European warrior with his axe in combat,

The uplifted arm, the clatter of blows on the helmeted head,
The death-howl, the limpsy tumbling body, the rush
  of friend and foe thither,
The siege of revolted lieges determin'd for liberty,
The summons to surrender, the battering at castle gates,
  the truce and parley,
The sack of an old city in its time,
The bursting in of mercenaries and bigots tumultuously and
  disorderly,
Roar, flames, blood, drunkenness, madness,
Goods freely rifled from houses and temples, screams
  of women in the gripe of brigands,
Craft and thievery of camp-followers, men running,
  old persons despairing,
The hell of war, the cruelties of creeds,
The list of all executive deeds and words just or unjust,
The power of personality just or unjust.

    4

Muscle and pluck forever!
What invigorates life invigorates death,
And the dead advance as much as the living advance,
And the future is no more uncertain than the present,
For the roughness of the earth and of man encloses as
      much as the delicatesse of the earth and of man,
And nothing endures but personal qualities.

What do you think endures?
Do you think a great city endures?
Or a teeming manufacturing state? or a prepared
      constitution? or the best built steamships?
Or hotels of granite and iron? or any chef-d'oeuvres of
      engineering, forts, armaments?
Away! these are not to be cherish'd for themselves,
They fill their hour, the dancers dance, the musicians play
      for them,

The show passes, all does well enough of course,
All does very well till one flash of defiance.

A great city is that which has the greatest men and women,
If it be a few ragged huts it is still the greatest city in the
whole world.

5

The place where a great city stands is not the place of
stretch'd wharves, docks, manufactures, deposits of
produce merely,
Nor the place of ceaseless salutes of new-comers or the
anchor-lifters of the departing,
Nor the place of the tallest and costliest buildings or
shops selling goods from the rest of the earth,
Nor the place of the best libraries and schools, nor the place
where money is plentiest,
Nor the place of the most numerous population.

Where the city stands with the brawniest breed of orators
and bards,
Where the city stands that is belov'd by these, and loves
them in return and understands them,
Where no monuments exist to heroes but in the
common words and deeds,
Where thrift is in its place, and prudence is in its place,
Where the men and women think lightly of the laws,
Where the slave ceases, and the master of slaves ceases,
Where the populace rise at once against the never-ending
audacity of elected persons,
Where fierce men and women pour forth as the sea to the
whistle of death pours its sweeping and unript waves,
Where outside authority enters always after the precedence
of inside authority.
Where the citizen is always the head and ideal, and
President, Mayor, Governor and what not, are
agents for pay.

Where children are taught to be laws to themselves, and
    to depend on themselves,
Where equanimity is illustrated in affairs,
Where speculations on the soul are encouraged,
Where women walk in public processions in the streets
    the same as the men,
Where they enter the public assembly and take places
    the same as the men,
Where the city of the faithfulest friends stands,
Where the city of the cleanliness of the sexes stands,
Where the city of the healthiest fathers stands,
Where the city of the best-bodied mothers stands,
There the great city stands.

6

How beggarly appear arguments before a defiant deed!
How the floridness of the materials of cities shrivels before
    a man's or woman's look!

All waits or goes by default till a strong being appears;
A strong being is the proof of the race and of the
    ability of the universe,
When he or she appears materials are overaw'd,
The dispute on the soul stops,
The old customs and phrases are confronted, turn'd back,
    or laid away.

What is your money-making now? what can it do now?
What is your respectability now?
What are your theology, tuition, society, traditions,
    statute-books, now?
Where are your jibes of being now?
Where are your cavils about the soul now?

7

A sterile landscape covers the ore, there is as good as the
    best for all the forbidding appearance.
There is the mine, there are the miners,
The forge-furnace is there, the melt is accomplish'd,
    the hammersmen are at hand with their tongs
    and hammers,
What always served and always serves is at hand.

Than this nothing has better served, it has served all,
Served the fluent-tongued and subtle-sensed Greek, and
    long ere the Greek,
Served in building the buildings that last longer than any,
Served the Hebrew, the Persian, the most ancient
    Hindustanee,
Served the mound-raiser on the Mississippi, served those
    whose relics remain in Central America,
Served Albic temples in woods or on plains, with unhewn
    pillars and the druids,
Served the artificial clefts, vast, high, silent, on the
    snow-cover'd hills of Scandinavia,
Served those who time out of mind made on the granite
    walls rough sketches of the sun, moon, stars, ships,
    ocean waves,
Served the paths of the irruptions of the Goths, served the
    pastoral tribes and nomads,
Served the long distant Kelt, served the hardy pirates of
    the Baltic,
Served before any of those the venerable and harmless
    men of Ethiopia,
Served the making of helms for the galleys of pleasure
    and the making of those for war,
Served all great works on land and all great works on the sea,
For the medieval ages and before the medieval ages,
Served not the living only then as now, but served the dead.

8

I see the European headsman,
He stands mask'd, clothed in red, with huge legs and
      strong naked arms,
And leans on a ponderous axe.

(Whom have you slaughter'd lately European headsman?
Whose is that blood upon you so wet and sticky?)

I see the clear sunset of the martyrs,
I see from the scaffolds the descending ghosts,
Ghosts of dead lords, uncrown'd ladies, impeach'd
      ministers, rejected kings,
Rivals, traitors, poisoners, disgraced chieftains and the rest.

I see those who in any land have died for the good cause,
The seed is spare, nevertheless the crop shall never run out,
(Mind you O foreign kings, O priests, the crop shall
      never run out.)

I see the blood wash'd entirely away from the axe,
Both blade and helve are clean,
They spirt no more the blood of European nobles, they
      clasp no more the necks of queens.

I see the headsman withdraw and become useless,
I see the scaffold untrodden and mouldy, I see no
      longer any axe upon it,
I see the mighty and friendly emblem of the power of my
      own race, the newest, largest race.

9

(America! I do not vaunt my love for you,
I have what I have.)

The axe leaps!
The solid forest gives fluid utterances,
They tumble forth, they rise and form,
Hut, tent, landing, survey,
Flail, plough, pick, crowbar, spade,
Shingle, rail, prop, wainscot, jamb, lath, panel, gable,
Citadel, ceiling, saloon, academy, organ, exhibition-house,
    library,
Cornice, trellis, pilaster, balcony, window, turret, porch,
Hoe, rake, pitchfork, pencil, wagon, staff, saw,
    jack-plane, mallet, wedge, rounce,
Chair, tub, hoop, table, wicket, vane, sash, floor,
Work-box, chest, string'd instrument, boat, frame, and
    what not,
Capitols of States, and capitol of the nation of States,
Long stately rows in avenues, hospitals for orphans or for
    the poor or sick,
Manhattan steamboats and clippers taking the measure of
    all seas.

The shapes arise!
Shapes of the using of axes anyhow, and the users and
    all that neighbors them,
Cutters down of wood and haulers of it to the
    Penobscot or Kennebec,
Dwellers in cabins among the California mountains
    or by the little lakes, or on the Columbia,
Dwellers south on the banks of the Gila or Rio Grande,
    friendly gatherings, the characters and fun,
Dwellers along the St. Lawrence, or north in Kanada, or
    down by the Yellowstone, dwellers on coasts
    and off coasts,
Seal-fishers, whalers, arctic seamen breaking passages
    through the ice.

The shapes arise!
Shapes of factories, arsenals, foundries, markets,
Shapes of the two-threaded tracks of railroads,
Shapes of the sleepers of bridges, vast frameworks, girders,
    arches,
Shapes of the fleets of barges, tows, lake and canal craft,
    river craft,
Ship-yards and dry-docks along the Eastern and
    Western seas, and in many a bay and by-place,
The live-oak kelsons, the pine planks, the spars, the
    hackmatack-roots for knees,
The ships themselves on their ways, the tiers of scaffolds,
    the workmen busy outside and inside,
The tools lying around, the great auger and little auger,
    the adze, bolt, line, square, gouge, and bead-plane.

10

The shapes arise!
The shape measur'd, saw'd, jack'd, join'd, stain'd,
The coffin-shape for the dead to lie within in his shroud,
The shape got out in posts, in the bedstead posts, in the
    posts of the bride's bed,
The shape of the little trough, the shape of the rockers
    beneath, the shape of the babe's cradle,
The shape of the floor-planks, the floor-planks for
    dancers' feet,
The shape of the planks of the family home, the home
    of the friendly parents and children,
The shape of the roof of the home of the happy young man
    and woman, the roof over the well-married young
    man and woman,
The roof over the supper joyously cook'd by the
    chaste wife, and joyously eaten by the chaste husband,
    content after his day's work.

The shapes arise!
The shape of the prisoner's place in the court-room,
    and of him or her seated in the place,
The shape of the liquor-bar lean'd against by the
    young rum-drinker and the old rum-drinker,
The shape of the shamed and angry stairs trod by
    sneaking footsteps,
The shape of the sly settee, and the adulterous
    unwholesome couple,
The shape of the gambling-board with its devilish
    winnings and losings,
The shape of the step-ladder for the convicted and
    sentenced murderer, the murderer with haggard
    face and pinion'd arms,
The sheriff at hand with his deputies, the silent and
    white-lipp'd crowd, the dangling of the rope.

The shapes arise!
Shapes of doors giving many exits and entrances,
The door passing the dissever'd friend flush'd and in haste,
The door that admits good news and bad news,
The door whence the son left home confident and puff'd up,
The door he enter'd again from a long and scandalous
    absence, diseas'd, broken down, without innocence,
    without means.

11
Her shape arises,
She less guarded than ever, yet more guarded than ever,
The gross and soil'd she moves among do not make her
    gross and soil'd,
She knows the thoughts as she passes, nothing is
    conceal'd from her,
She is none the less considerate or friendly therefor,
She is the best belov'd, it is without exception, she has
    no reason to fear and she does not fear,

Oaths, quarrels, hiccup'd songs, smutty expressions,
    are idle to her as she passes,
She is silent, she is possess'd of herself, they do not offend her,
She receives them as the laws of Nature receive them,
    she is strong,
She too is a law of Nature—there is no law stronger than
    she is.

12
The main shapes arise!
Shapes of Democracy total, result of centuries,
Shapes ever projecting other shapes,
Shapes of turbulent manly cities,
Shapes of the friends and home-givers of the whole earth,
Shapes bracing the earth and braced with the whole earth.

                          [1856]

THIS COMPOST

1
Something startles me where I thought I was safest,
I withdraw from the still woods I loved,
I will not go now on the pastures to walk,
I will not strip the clothes from my body to meet my lover
    the sea,
I will not touch my flesh to the earth as to other flesh
    to renew me.

O how can it be that the ground itself does not sicken?
How can you be alive you growths of spring?

How can you furnish health you blood of herbs, roots,
    orchards, grain?
Are they not continually putting distemper'd corpses
    within you?
Is not every continent work'd over and over with sour dead?

Where have you disposed of their carcasses?
Those drunkards and gluttons of so many generations?
Where have you drawn off all the foul liquid and meat?
I do not see any of it upon you to-day, or perhaps
    I am deceiv'd,
I will run a furrow with my plough, I will press my
    spade through the sod and turn it up underneath,
I am sure I shall expose some of the foul meat.

2

Behold this compost! behold it well!
Perhaps every mite has once form'd part of a sick
    person—yet behold!
The grass of spring covers the prairies,
The bean bursts noiselessly through the mould in the garden,
The delicate spear of the onion pierces upward,
The apple-buds cluster together on the apple-branches,
The resurrection of the wheat appears with pale visage
    out of its graves,
The tinge awakes over the willow-tree and the mulberry-tree,
The he-birds carol mornings and evenings while the
    she-birds sit on their nests,
The young of poultry break through the hatch'd eggs,
The new-born of animals appear, the calf is dropt from
    the cow, the colt from the mare,
Out of its little hill faithfully rise the potato's dark green
    leaves,
Out of its hill rises the yellow maize-stalk, the lilacs
    bloom in the dooryards,
The summer growth is innocent and disdainful
    above all those strata of sour dead.

What chemistry!
That the winds are really not infectious,
That this is no cheat, this transparent green-wash
    of the sea which is so amorous after me,
That it is safe to allow it to lick my naked body all over
    with its tongues,
That it will not endanger me with the fevers that have
    deposited themselves in it,
That all is clean forever and forever,
That the cool drink from the well tastes so good,
That blackberries are so flavorous and juicy,
That the fruits of the apple-orchard and the orange-orchard,
    that melons, grapes, peaches, plums, will none
    of them poison me,
That when I recline on the grass I do not catch any disease,
Though probably every spear of grass rises out of what
    was once a catching disease.

Now I am terrified at the Earth, it is that calm and patient,
It grows such sweet things out of such corruptions,
It turns harmless and stainless on its axis, with such
    endless successions of diseas'd corpses,
It distills such exquisite winds out of such infused fetor,
It renews with such unwitting looks its prodigal,
    annual, sumptuous crops,
It gives such divine materials to men, and accepts
    such leavings from them at last.

                        [1856]

CROSSING BROOKLYN FERRY

1

Flood-tide below me! I see you face to face!
Clouds of the west—sun there half an hour high—I see you
    also face to face.

Crowds of men and women attired in the usual costumes,
    how curious you are to me!
On the ferry-boats the hundreds and hundreds that
    cross, returning home, are more curious to me
    than you suppose,
And you that shall cross from shore to shore years hence
    are more to me, and more in my meditations, than you
    might suppose.

2

The impalpable sustenance of me from all things at all
    hours of the day,
The simple, compact, well-join'd scheme, myself
    disintegrated, every one disintegrated yet part of
    the scheme,
The similitudes of the past and those of the future,
The glories strung like beads on my smallest sights and
    hearings, on the walk in the street and the passage
    over the river,
The current rushing so swiftly and swimming with me
    far away,
The others that are to follow me, the ties between
    me and them,
The certainty of others, the life, love, sight, hearing of
    others.

Others will enter the gates of the ferry and cross from shore
    to shore,
Others will watch the run of the flood-tide,
Others will see the shipping of Manhattan north and west,
    and the heights of Brooklyn to the south and east,
Others will see the islands large and small;
Fifty years hence, others will see them as they cross,
    the sun half an hour high,
A hundred years hence, or ever so many hundred years
    hence, others will see them,
Will enjoy the sunset, the pouring-in of the flood-tide,
    the falling-back to the sea of the ebb-tide.

3

It avails not, time nor place—distance avails not,
I am with you, you men and women of a generation,
    or ever so many generations hence,
Just as you feel when you look on the river and sky,
    so I felt,
Just as any of you is one of a living crowd, I was
    one of a crowd,
Just as you are refresh'd by the gladness of the river and the
    bright flow, I was refresh'd,
Just as you stand and lean on the rail, yet hurry with the
    swift current, I stood yet was hurried,
Just as you look on the numberless masts of ships
    and the thick-stemm'd pipes of steamboats, I look'd.
I too many and many a time cross'd the river of old,
Watched the Twelfth-month sea-gulls, saw them high
    in the air floating with motionless wings, oscillating
    their bodies,
Saw how the glistening yellow lit up parts of their
    bodies and left the rest in strong shadow,
Saw the slow-wheeling circles and the gradual edging
    toward the south,

Saw the reflection of the summer sky in the water,
Had my eyes dazzled by the shimmering track of beams,
Look'd at the fine centrifugal spokes of light round the
     shape of my head in the sunlit water,
Look'd on the haze on the hills southward and
     south-westward,
Look'd on the vapor as it flew in fleeces tinged with violet,
Look'd toward the lower bay to notice the vessels arriving,
Saw their approach, saw aboard those that were near me,
Saw the white sails of schooners and sloops, saw the
     ships at anchor,
The sailors at work in the rigging or out astride the spars,
The round masts, the swinging motion of the hulls, the
     slender serpentine pennants,
The large and small steamers in motion, the pilots in
     their pilot-houses,
The white wake left by the passage, the quick tremulous
     whirl of the wheels,
The flags of all nations, the falling of them at sunset,
The scallop-edged waves in the twilight, the ladled cups,
     the frolicsome crests and glistening,
The stretch afar growing dimmer and dimmer, the gray
     walls of the granite storehouses by the docks,
On the river the shadowy group, the big steam-tug
     closely flank'd on each side by the barges, the hay-boat,
     the belated lighter,
On the neighboring shore the fires from the foundry
     chimneys burning high and glaringly into the night,
Casting their flicker of black contrasted with wild
     red and yellow light over the tops of houses, and
     down into the clefts of streets.

     4
These and all else were to me the same as they are to you,
I loved well those cities, loved well the stately and rapid river,
The men and women I saw were all near to me,

Others the same—others who look back on me because
    I look'd forward to them,
(The time will come, though I stop here to-day and to-night.)

5

What is it then between us?
What is the count of the scores or hundreds of years
    between us?

Whatever it is, it avails not—distance avails not,
    and place avails not,
I too lived, Brooklyn of ample hills was mine,
I too walk'd the streets of Manhattan island, and bathed
    in the waters around it,
I too felt the curious abrupt questionings stir within me,
In the day among crowds of people sometimes they came
    upon me,
In my walks home late at night or as I lay in my bed
    they came upon me,
I too had been struck from the float forever held in solution,
I too had receiv'd identity by my body,
That I was I knew was of my body, and what I should
    be I knew I should be of my body.

6

It is not upon you alone the dark patches fall,
The dark threw its patches down upon me also,
The best I had done seem'd to me blank and suspicious,
My great thoughts as I supposed them, were they not
    in reality meagre?
Nor is it you alone who know what it is to be evil,
I am he who knew what it was to be evil,
I too knitted the old knot of contrariety,
Blabb'd, blush'd, resented, lied, stole, grudg'd,
Had guile, anger, lust, hot wishes I dared not speak,
Was wayward, vain, greedy, shallow, sly, cowardly, malignant,

The wolf, the snake, the hog, not wanting in me,
The cheating look, the frivolous word, the adulterous
    wish, not wanting.
Refusals, hates, postponements, meanness, laziness, none
    of these wanting,
Was one with the rest, the days and haps of the rest,
Was call'd by my nighest name by clear loud voices of
    young men as they saw me approaching or passing,
Felt their arms on my neck as I stood, or the negligent
    leaning of their flesh against me as I sat,
Saw many I loved in the street or ferry-boat or public
    assembly, yet never told them a word,
Lived the same life with the rest, the same old laughing,
    gnawing, sleeping,
Play'd the part that still looks back on the actor or actress,
The same old role, the role that is what we make it,
    as great as we like,
Or as small as we like, or both great and small.

7

Closer yet I approach you,
What thought you have of me now, I had as much of you—
    I laid in my stores in advance,
I consider'd long and seriously of you before you were born.

Who was to know what should come home to me?
Who knows but I am enjoying this?
Who knows, for all the distance, but I am as good as
    looking at you now, for all you cannot see me?

8

Ah, what can ever be more stately and admirable to me
    than mast-hemm'd Manhattan?
River and sunset and scallop-edg'd waves of flood-tide?
The sea-gulls oscillating their bodies, the hay-boat
    in the twilight, and the belated lighter?

What gods can exceed these that clasp me by the hand, and
    with voices I love call me promptly and loudly by
    my nighest name as I approach?
What is more subtle than this which ties me to the
    woman or man that looks in my face?
Which fuses me into you now, and pours my meaning
    into you?

We understand then do we not?
What I promis'd without mentioning it, have you not
    accepted?
What the study could not teach—what the preaching
    could not accomplish is accomplish'd, is it not?

9
Flow on, river! flow with the flood-tide, and ebb with
    the ebb-tide!
Frolic on, crested and scallop-edg'd waves!
Gorgeous clouds of the sunset! drench with your splendor
    me, or the men and women generations after me!
Cross from shore to shore, countless crowds of passengers!
Stand up, tall masts of Mannahatta! stand up, beautiful
    hills of Brooklyn!
Throb, baffled and curious brain! throw out questions
    and answers!
Suspend here and everywhere, eternal float of solution!
Gaze, loving and thirsting eyes, in the house or street or
    public assembly!
Sound out, voices of young men? loudly and musically
    call me by my nighest name!
Live, old life! play the part that looks back on the
    actor or actress!
Play the old role, the role that is great or small according
    as one makes it!
Consider, you who peruse me, whether I may not in
    unknown ways be looking upon you;

Be firm, rail over the river, to support those who lean idly,
    yet haste with the hasting current;
Fly on, sea-birds! fly sideways, or wheel in large circles
    high in the air;
Receive the summer sky, you water, and faithfully hold it
    till all downcast eyes have time to take it from you!

Diverge, fine spokes of light, from the shape of my head,
    or any one's head, in the sunlit water!
Come on, ships from the lower bay! pass up or down,
    white-sail'd schooners, sloops, lighters!
Flaunt away, flags of all nations! be duly lower'd at sunset!
Burn high your fires, foundry chimneys! cast black
    shadows at nightfall! cast red and yellow light over
    the tops of the houses!
Appearances, now or henceforth, indicate what you are,
You necessary film, continue to envelop the soul,
About my body for me, and your body for you, be
    hung our divest aromas,
Thrive, cities—bring your freight, bring your shows, ample
    and sufficient rivers,
Expand, being than which none else is perhaps more
    spiritual,
Keep your places, objects than which none else is
    more lasting.

You have waited, you always wait, you dumb, beautiful
    ministers,
We receive you with free sense at last, and are insatiate
    henceforward,
Not you any more shall be able to foil us, or withhold
    yourselves from us,
We use you, and do not cast you aside—we plant
    you permanently within us,

We fathom you not—we love you—there is perfection
    in you also,
You furnish your parts toward eternity,
Great or small, you furnish your parts toward the soul.

                                         [1856]

SONG OF THE OPEN ROAD

1

Afoot and light-hearted I take to the open road,
Healthy, free, the world before me,
The long brown path before me leading wherever I choose.

Henceforth I ask not good-fortune, I myself am good-fortune,
Henceforth I whimper no more, postpone no more, need
    nothing,
Done with indoor complaints, libraries, querulous criticisms,
Strong and content I travel the open road.

The earth, that is sufficient,
I do not want the constellations any nearer,
I know they are very well where they are,
I know they suffice for those who belong to them.

(Still here I carry my old delicious burdens,
I carry them, men and women, I carry them with me
    wherever I go,
I swear it is impossible for me to get rid of them,
I am fill'd with them, and I will fill them in return.)

2

You road I enter upon and look around, I believe you are
  not all that is here,
I believe that much unseen is also here.

Here the profound lesson of reception, nor preference
  nor denial,
The black with his woolly head, the felon, the diseas'd,
  the illiterate person, are not denied;
The birth, the hasting after the physician, the beggar's
  tramp, the drunkard's stagger, the laughing party of
  mechanics,
The escaped youth, the rich person's carriage, the fop,
  the eloping couple,
The early market-man, the hearse, the moving of furniture
  into the town, the return back from the town,
They pass, I also pass, any thing passes, none can be
  interdicted,
None but are accepted, none but shall be dear to me.

3

You air that serves me with breath to speak!
You objects that call from diffusion my meanings and
  give them shape!
You light that wraps me and all things in delicate
  equable showers!
You paths worn in the irregular hollows by the roadsides!
I believe you are latent with unseen existences, you are
  so dear to me.

You flagg'd walks of the cities! you strong curbs at
  the edges!
You ferries! you planks and posts of wharves! you
  timber-lined sides! you distant ships!
You rows of houses! you window-pierc'd facades! you roofs!
You porches and entrances! you copings and iron guards!

You windows whose transparent shells might expose
    so much!
You doors and ascending steps! you arches!
You gray stones of interminable pavements! you trodden
    crossings!
From all that has touch'd you I believe you have
    imparted to yourselves, and now would impart the
    same secretly to me,
From the living and the dead you have peopled
    your impassive surfaces, and the spirits thereof would
    be evident and amicable with me.

    4
The earth expanding right hand and left hand,
The picture alive, every part in its best light,
The music falling in where it is wanted, and stopping where
    it is not wanted,
The cheerful voice of the public road, the gay fresh
    sentiment of the road.

O highway I travel, do you say to me *Do not leave me?*
Do you say *Venture not—if you leave me you are lost?*
Do you say *I am already prepared, I am well-beaten
    and undenied, adhere to me?*

O public road, I say back I am not afraid to leave you,
    yet I love you,
You express me better than I can express myself,
You shall be more to me than my poem.

I think heroic deeds were all conceiv'd in the open air, and
    all free poems also,
I think I could stop here myself and do miracles,
I think whatever I shall meet on the road I shall like,
    and whoever beholds me shall like me,
I think whoever I see must be happy.

5

From this hour I ordain myself loos'd of limits and
    imaginary lines,
Going where I list, my own master total and absolute,
Listening to others, considering well what they say,
Pausing, searching, receiving, contemplating,
Gently, but with undeniable will, divesting myself of the
    holds that would hold me.

I inhale great draughts of space,
The east and the west are mine, and the north and
    the south are mine.

I am larger, better than I thought,
I did not know I held so much goodness.

All seems beautiful to me,
I can repeat over to men and women You have done such
    good to me I would do the same to you,
I will recruit for myself and you as I go,
I will scatter myself among men and women as I go,
I will toss a new gladness and roughness among them,
Whoever denies me it shall not trouble me,
Whoever accepts me he or she shall be blessed and shall
    bless me.

6

Now if a thousand perfect men were to appear it would not
    amaze me,
Now if a thousand beautiful forms of women appear'd
    it would not astonish me.

Now I see the secret of the making of the best persons,
It is to grow in the open air and to eat and sleep with the earth.
Here a great personal deed has room,
(Such a deed seizes upon the hearts of the whole race of men,

Its effusion of strength and will overwhelms law and
     mocks all authority and all argument against it.)

Here is the test of wisdom,
Wisdom is not finally tested in schools,
Wisdom cannot be pass'd from one having it to
     another not having it,
Wisdom is of the soul, is not susceptible of proof, is its
     own proof,
Applies to all stages and objects and qualities and is content,
Is the certainty of the reality and immortality of things, and
     the excellence of things;
Something there is in the float of the sight of things
     that provokes it out of the soul.

Now I re-examine philosophies and religions,
They may prove well in lecture-rooms, yet not prove
     at all under the spacious clouds and along the landscape
     and flowing currents.

Here is realization,
Here is a man tallied—he realizes here what he has in him,
The past, the future, majesty, love—if they are vacant
     of you, you are vacant of them.

Only the kernel of every object nourishes;
Where is he who tears off the husks for you and me?
Where is he that undoes stratagems and envelopes
     for you and me?

Here is adhesiveness, it is not previously fashion'd, it is apropos;
Do you know what it is as you pass to be loved by strangers?
Do you know the talk of those turning eye-balls?

7

Here is the efflux of the soul,
The efflux of the soul comes from within through
    embower'd gates, ever provoking questions,
These yearnings why are they? these thoughts in the
    darkness why are they?
Why are there men and women that while they are nigh
    me the sunlight expands my blood?
Why when they leave me do my pennants of joy sink flat
    and lank?
Why are there trees I never walk under but large and
    melodious thoughts descend upon me?
(I think they hang there winter and summer on
    those trees and always drop fruit as I pass;)
What is it I interchange so suddenly with strangers?
What with some driver as I ride on the seat by his side?
What with some fisherman drawing his seine by the
    shore as I walk by and pause?
What gives me to be free to a woman's and man's
    good-will? what gives them to be free to mine?

8

The efflux of the soul is happiness, here is happiness,
I think it pervades the open air, waiting at all times,
Now it flows unto us, we are rightly charged.

Here rises the fluid and attaching character,
The fluid and attaching character is the freshness and
    sweetness of man and woman,
(The herbs of the morning sprout no fresher and sweeter
    every day out of the roots of themselves, than it sprouts
    fresh and sweet continually out of itself.)

Toward the fluid and attaching character exudes the sweat
    of the love of young and old,

From it falls distill'd the charm that mocks beauty and
    attainments,
Toward it heaves the shuddering longing ache of contact.

9

Allons! whoever you are come travel with me!
Traveling with me you find what never tires.

The earth never tires,
The earth is rude, silent, incomprehensible at first, Nature
    is rude and incomprehensible at first,
Be not discouraged, keep on, there are divine things
    well envelop'd,
I swear to you there are divine things more beautiful
    than words can tell.

Allons! we must not stop here,
However sweet these laid-up stores, however convenient
    this dwelling we cannot remain here,
However shelter'd this port and however calm these
    waters we must not anchor here,
However welcome the hospitality that surrounds us
    we are permitted to receive it but a little while.

10

Allons! the inducements shall be greater,
We will sail pathless and wild seas,
We will go where winds blow, waves dash, and the Yankee
    clipper speeds by under full sail.

Allons! with power, liberty, the earth, the elements,
Health, defiance, gayety, self-esteem, curiosity;
Allons! from all formules!
From your formules, O bat-eyed and materialistic priests.

The stale cadaver blocks up the passage—the burial waits
    no longer.

Allons! yet take warning!
He traveling with me needs the best blood, thews, endurance,
None may come to the trial till he or she bring courage
and health,
Come not here if you have already spent the best of yourself,
Only those may come who come in sweet and determin'd
bodies,
No diseas'd person, no rum drinker or venereal taint
is permitted here.

(I and mine do not convince by arguments, similes, rhymes,
We convince by our presence.)

11

Listen! I will be honest with you,
I do not offer the old smooth prizes, but offer rough
new prizes,
These are the days that must happen to you:
You shall not heap up what is call'd riches,
You shall scatter with lavish hand all that you earn or
achieve,
You but arrive at the city to which you were destin'd,
you hardly settle yourself to satisfaction before
you are call'd by an irresistible call to depart,
You shall be treated to the ironical smiles and mockings
of those who remain behind you,
What beckonings of love you receive you shall only answer
with passionate kisses of parting,
You shall not allow the hold of those who spread their
reach'd hands toward you.

12

Allons! after the great Companions, and to belong to
them!
They too are on the road—they are the swift and majestic
men—they are the greatest women,
Enjoyers of calms of seas and storms of seas,
Sailors of many a ship, walkers of many a mile of land,

Habituès of many distant countries, habituès of far-distant
    dwellings,
Trusters of men and women, observers of cities, solitary
    toilers,
Pausers and contemplators of tufts, blossoms, shells
    of the shore,
Dancers at wedding-dances, kissers of brides, tender
    helpers of children, bearers of children,
Soldiers of revolts, standers by gaping graves,
    lowerers-down of coffins,
Journeyers over consecutive seasons, over the years,
    the curious years each emerging from that
    which preceded it,
Journeyers as with companions, namely their own diverse
    phases,
Forth-steppers from the latent unrealized baby-days,
Journeyers gayly with their own youth, journeyers with
    their bearded and well-grain'd manhood,
Journeyers with their womanhood, ample, unsurpass'd,
    content,
Journeyers with their own sublime old age of manhood
    or womanhood,
Old age, calm, expanded, broad with the haughty breadth
    of the universe,
Old age, flowing free with the delicious near-by freedom
    of death.

13

Allons! to that which is endless as it was beginningless,
To undergo much, tramps of days, rests of nights,
To merge all in the travel they tend to, and the days
    and nights they tend to,
Again to merge them in the start of superior journeys,
To see nothing anywhere but what you may reach it and
    pass it,
To conceive no time, however distant, but what you
    may reach it and pass it,

To look up or down no road but it stretches and waits for
    you, however long but it stretches and waits for you,
To see no being, not God's or any, but you also go thither,
To see no possession but you may possess it, enjoying
    all without labor or purchase, abstracting the feast
    yet not abstracting one particle of it,
To take the best of the farmer's farm and the rich
    man's elegant villa, and the chaste blessings of the
    well-married couple, and the fruits of orchards
    and flowers of gardens,
To take to your use out of the compact cities as you pass
    through,
To carry buildings and streets with you afterward
    wherever you go,
To gather the minds of men out of their brains as you
    encounter them, to gather the love out of their hearts,
To take your lovers on the road with you, for all that
    you leave them behind you,
To know the universe itself as a road, as many roads, as
    roads for traveling souls.

All parts away for the progress of souls,
All religion, all solid things, arts, governments—all that
    was or is apparent upon this globe or any globe,
    falls into niches and corners before the procession
    of souls along the grand roads of the universe.

Of the progress of the souls of men and women along
    the grand roads of the universe, all other progress is the
    needed emblem and sustenance.

Forever alive, forever forward,
Stately, solemn, sad, withdrawn, baffled, mad, turbulent,
    feeble, dissatisfied,
Desperate, proud, fond, sick, accepted by men, rejected
    by men,

They go! they go! I know that they go, but I know
    not where they go,
But I know that they go toward the best—toward
    something great.

Whoever you are, come forth! or man or woman come forth!
You must not stay sleeping and dallying there in the house,
    though you built it, or though it has been built for you.
Out of the dark confinement! out from behind the screen!
It is useless to protest, I know all and expose it.

Behold through you as bad as the rest,
Through the laughter, dancing, dining, supping, of people,
Inside of dresses and ornaments, inside of those wash'd
    and trimm'd faces,
Behold a secret silent loathing and despair.

No husband, no wife, no friend, trusted to hear the
    confession,
Another self, a duplicate of every one, skulking and
    hiding it goes,
Formless and wordless through the streets of the cities,
    polite and bland in the parlors,
In the cars of railroads, in steamboats, in the public
    assembly,
Home to the houses of men and women, at the table,
    in the bedroom, everywhere,
Smartly attired, countenance smiling, form upright, death
    under the breast-bones, hell under the skull-bones,
Under the broadcloth and gloves, under the ribbons and
    artificial flowers,
Keeping fair with the customs, speaking not a syllable
    of itself,
Speaking of any thing else but never of itself.

14

Allons! through struggles and wars!
The goal that was named cannot be countermanded.

Have the past struggles succeeded?
What has succeeded? yourself? your nation? Nature?
Now understand me well—it is provided in the essence
    of things that from any fruition of success, no
    matter what, shall come forth something to make
    a greater struggle necessary.

My call is the call of battle, I nourish active rebellion,
He going with me must go well arm'd,
He going with me goes often with spare diet, poverty,
    angry enemies, desertions.

15

Allons! the road is before us!
It is safe—I have tried it—my own feet have tried
    it well—be not detain'd!
Let the paper remain on the desk unwritten, and the
    book on the self unopen'd!
Let the tools remain in the workshop! let the
    money remain unearn'd!
Let the school stand! mind not the cry of the teacher!
Let the preacher preach in his pulpit! let the lawyer
    plead in the court, and the judge expound the law.

Camerado, I give you my hand!
I give you my love more precious than money,
I give you myself before preaching or law;
Will you give me yourself? will you come travel with me?
Shall we stick by each other as long as we-live?

[1856]

A WOMAN WAITS FOR ME

A woman waits for me, she contains all, nothing is lacking,
Yet all were lacking if sex were lacking, or if the moisture
    of the right man were lacking.

Sex contains all, bodies, souls,
Meanings, proofs, purities, delicacies, results, promulgations,
Songs, commands, health, pride, the maternal mystery,
    the seminal milk,
All hopes, benefactions, bestowals, all the passions,
    loves, beauties, delights of the earth,
All the governments, judges, gods, follow'd persons of
    the earth,
These are contain'd in sex as parts of itself and justifications
    of itself.

Without shame the man I like knows and avows the
    deliciousness of his sex,
Without shame the woman I like knows and avows hers.

Now I will dismiss myself from impassive women,
I will go stay with her who waits for me, and with those
    women that are warm-blooded and sufficient for me,
I see that they understand me and do not deny me,
I see that they are worthy of me, I will be the robust
    husband of those women.

They are not one jot less than I am,
They are tann'd in the face by shining suns and blowing
    winds,
Their flesh has the old divine suppleness and strength,
They know how to swim, row, ride, wrestle, shoot, run,
    strike, retreat, advance, resist, defend themselves,

They are ultimate in their own right—they are calm,
    clear, well-possess'd of themselves.

I draw you close to me, you women,
I cannot let you go, I would do you good,
I am for you, and you are for me, not only for our own sake,
    but for others' sakes,
Envelop'd in you sleep greater heroes and bards,
They refuse to awake at the touch of any man but me.

It is I, you women, I make my way,
I am stern, acrid, large, undissuadable, but I love you,
I do not hurt you any more than is necessary for you,
I pour the stuff to start sons and daughters fit for these
    States, I press with slow rude muscle,
I brace myself effectually, I listen to no entreaties,
I dare not withdraw till I deposit what has so long
    accumulated within me.

Through you I drain the pent-up rivers of myself,
In you I wrap a thousand onward years,
On you I graft the grafts of the best-loved of me and
    America,
The drops I distil upon you shall grow fierce and
    athletic girls, new artists, musicians, and singers,
The babes I beget upon you are to beget babes in their turn,
I shall demand perfect men and women out of my
    love-spendings,
I shall expect them to interpenetrate with others,
    as I and you interpenetrate now,
I shall count on the fruits of the gushing showers of them,
    as I count on the fruits of the gushing showers
    I give now,
I shall look for loving crops from the birth, life, death,
    immortality, I plant so lovingly now.

                     [1856]

ON THE BEACH AT NIGHT ALONE

On the beach at night alone,
As the old mother sways her to and fro singing her
husky song,
As I watch the bright stars shining, I think a thought of
the clef of the universes and of the future.

A vast similitude interlocks all,
All spheres, grown, ungrown, small, large, suns, moons,
planets,
All distances of place however wide,
All distances of time, all inanimate forms,
All souls, all living bodies though they be ever so different,
or in different worlds,
All gaseous, watery, vegetable, mineral processes, the
fishes, the brutes,
All nations, colors, barbarisms, civilizations, languages,
All identities that have existed or may exist on this
globe or any globe,
All lives and deaths, all of the past, present, future,
This vast similitude spans them, and always has spann'd,
And shall forever span them and compactly hold and
enclose them.

[1856]

TO A FOIL'D EUROPEAN REVOLUTIONAIRE

Courage yet, my brother or my sister!
Keep on—Liberty is to be subserv'd whatever occurs;
That is nothing that is quell'd by one or two failures, or
    any number of failures,
Or by the indifference or ingratitude of the people,
    or by any unfaithfulness,
Or the show of the tushes of power, soldiers, cannon,
    penal statutes.

What we believe in waits latent forever through
    all the continents,
Invites no one, promises nothing, sits in calmness and light,
    is positive and composed, knows no discouragement,
Waiting patiently, waiting its time.

(Not songs of loyalty alone are these,
But songs of insurrection also,
For I am the sworn poet of every dauntless rebel the
    world over,
And he going with me leaves peace and routine behind him,
And stakes his life to be lost at any moment.)

The battle rages with many a loud alarm and frequent
    advance and retreat,
The infidel triumphs, or supposes he triumphs,
The prison, scaffold, garroté, handcuffs, iron necklace
    and leadballs do their work,
The named and unnamed heroes pass to other spheres,
The great speakers and writers are exiled, they lie sick
    in distant lands,
The cause is asleep, the strongest throats are choked
    with their own blood,

The young men droop their eyelashes toward the ground
 when they meet;
But for all this Liberty has not gone out of the place,
 nor the infidel enter'd into full possession.

When liberty goes out of a place it is not the first to
 go, nor the second or third to go,
It waits for all the rest to go, it is the last.

When there are no more memories of heroes and martyrs,
And when all life and all the souls of men and women
 are discharged from any part of the earth,
Then only shall liberty or the idea of liberty be discharged
 from that part of the earth,
And the infidel come into full possession.

Then courage European revolter, revoltress!
For till all ceases neither must you cease.

I do not know what you are for. (I do not know what
 I am for myself, nor what any thing is for,)
But I will search carefully for it even in being foil'd,
In defeat, poverty, misconception, imprisonment—for they
 too are great.

Did we think victory great?
So it is—but now it seems to me, when it cannot be
 help'd, that defeat is great,
And that death and dismay are great.

           [1856]

OUT OF THE CRADLE ENDLESSLY ROCKING

Out of the cradle endlessly rocking,
Out of the mocking-bird's throat, the musical shuttle,
Out of the Ninth-month midnight,
Over the sterile sands and the fields beyond, where the child
    leaving his bed wander'd alone, bareheaded, barefoot,
Down from the shower'd halo,
Up from the mystic play of shadows twining and twisting
    as if they were alive,
Out from the patches of briers and blackberries,
From the memories of the bird that chanted to me,
From your memories sad brother, from the fitful risings
    and fallings I heard,
From under that yellow half-moon late-risen and
    swollen as if with tears,
From those beginning notes of yearning and love there
    in the mist,
From the thousand responses of my heart never to cease,
From the myriad thence-arous'd words,
From the word stronger and more delicious than any,
From such as now they start the scene revisiting,
As a flock, twittering, rising, or overhead passing,
Borne hither, ere all eludes me, hurriedly,
A man, yet by these tears a little boy again,
Throwing myself on the sand, confronting the waves,
I, chanter of pains and joys, uniter of here and hereafter,
Taking all hints to use them, but swiftly leaping
    beyond them,
A reminiscence sing.

Once Paumanok,
When the lilac-scent was in the air and Fifth-month
    grass was growing,
Up this seashore in some briers,
Two feather'd guests from Alabama, two together,
And their nest, and four light-green eggs spotted
    with brown,
And every day the he-bird to and fro near at hand,
And every day the she-bird crouch'd on her nest, silent,
    with bright eyes,
And every day I, a curious boy, never too close,
    never disturbing them,
Cautiously peering, absorbing, translating.

Shine! shine! shine!
Pour down your warmth, great sun!
While we bask, we two together.

Two together!
Winds blow south, or winds blow north,
Day come white, or night come black,
Home, or rivers and mountains from home,
Singing all time, minding no time,
While we two keep together.

Till of a sudden,
May-be kill'd, unknown to her mate,
One forenoon the she-bird crouch'd not on the nest,
Nor return'd that afternoon, nor the next,
Nor ever appear'd again.

And thenceforward all summer in the sound of the sea,
And at night under the full of the moon in calmer weather,
Over the hoarse surging of the sea,
Or flitting from brier to brier by day,
I saw, I heard at intervals the remaining one, the he-bird,
The solitary guest from Alabama.

Blow! blow! blow!
Blow up sea-winds along Paumanok's shore;
I wait and I wait till you blow my mate to me.

Yes, when the stars glisten'd,
All night long on the prong of a moss-scallop'd stake,
Down almost amid the slapping waves,
Sat the lone singer wonderful causing tears.

He call'd on his mate,
He pour'd forth the meanings which I of all men know.

Yes my brother I know,
The rest might not, but I have treasur'd every note,
For more than once dimly down to the beach gliding,
Silent, avoiding the moonbeams, blending myself with the
    shadows,
Recalling now the obscure shapes, the echoes, the
    sounds and sights after their sorts,
The white arms out in the breakers tirelessly tossing,
I, with bare feet, a child, the wind wafting my hair,
Listen'd long and long.

Listen'd to keep, to sing, now translating the notes,
Following you my brother.

Soothe! soothe! soothe!
Close on its wave soothes the wave behind,
And again another behind embracing and lapping, every
    one close,
But my love soothes not me, not me.

Low hangs the moon, it rose late,
It is lagging—O I think it is heavy with love, with love.

O madly the sea pushes upon the land,
With love, with love.

O night! do I not see my love fluttering out among the
*   breakers?*
What is that little black thing I see there in the white?

Loud! loud! loud!
Loud I call to you, my love!

High and clear I shoot my voice over the waves,
Surely you must know who is here, is here,
You must know who I am, my love.

Low-hanging moon!
What is that dusky spot in your brown yellow?
O it is the shape, the shape of my mate!
O moon do not keep her from me any longer.

Land! land! O land!
Whichever way I turn, O I think you could give me
*   my mate back again if you only would,*
For I am almost sure I see her dimly whichever way I look.

O rising stars!
Perhaps the one I want so much will rise, will rise
*   with some of you.*

O throat! O trembling throat!
Sound clearer through the atmosphere!
Pierce the woods, the earth,
Somewhere listening to catch you must be the one I want.

Shake out carols!
Solitary here, the night's carols!
Carols of lonesome love! death's carols!
Carols under that lagging, yellow, waning moon!
O under that moon where she droops almost down
*   into the sea!*
O reckless despairing carols.

But soft! sink low!
Soft! let me just murmur,
And do you wait a moment you husky-nois'd sea,
For somewhere I believe I heard my mate responding to me,
So faint, I must be still, be still to listen,
But not altogether still, for then she might not come
        immediately to me.

Hither my love!
Here I am! here!
With this just-sustain'd note I announce myself to you,
This gentle call is for you my love, for you.

Do not be decoy'd elsewhere,
That is the whistle of the wind, it is not my voice,
That is the fluttering, the fluttering of the spray,
Those are the shadows of leaves.

O darkness! O in vain!
O I am very sick and sorrowful.

O brown halo in the sky near the moon, drooping upon
        the sea!
O troubled reflection in the sea!
O throat! O throbbing heart!
And I singing uselessly, uselessly all the night.

O past! O happy life! O songs of joy!
In the air, in the woods, over fields,
Loved! loved! loved! loved! loved!
But my mate no more, no more with me!
We two together no more.

The aria sinking,
All else continuing, the stars shining,
The winds blowing, the notes of the bird continuous
        echoing,

With angry moans the fierce old mother incessantly moaning,
On the sands of Paumanok's shore gray and rustling,
The yellow half-moon enlarged, sagging down, drooping,
    the face of the sea almost touching,
The boy ecstatic, with his bare feet the waves, with
    his hair the atmosphere dallying,
The love in the heart long pent, now loose, now at
    last tumultuously bursting,
The aria's meaning, the ears, the soul, swiftly depositing,
The strange tears down the cheeks coursing,
The colloquy there, the trio, each uttering,
The undertone, the savage old mother incessantly crying,
To the boy's soul's questions sullenly timing, some drown'd
    secret hissing.
To the outsetting bard.

Demon or bird! (said the boy's soul,)
Is it indeed toward your mate you sing? or is it really to me?
For I, that was a child, my tongue's use sleeping,
    now I have heard you,
Now in a moment I know what I am for, I awake,
And already a thousand singers, a thousand songs, clearer,
    louder and more sorrowful than yours,
A thousand warbling echoes have started to life
    within me, never to die.

O you singer solitary, singing by yourself, projecting me,
O solitary me listening, never more shall I cease
    perpetuating you,
Never more shall I escape, never more the reverberations,
Never more the cries of unsatisfied love be absent from me,
Never again leave me to be the peaceful child I was
    before what there in the night,
By the sea under the yellow and sagging moon,
The messenger there arous'd, the fire, the sweet hell within,
The unknown want, the destiny of me.

O give me the clew! (it lurks in the night here somewhere,)
O if I am to have so much, let me have more!

A word then, (for I will conquer it,)
The word final, superior to all,
Subtle, sent up—what is it?—I listen;
Are you whispering it, and have been all the time,
        you sea-waves?
Is that it from your liquid rims and wet sands?

Whereto answering, the sea,
Delaying not, hurrying not,
Whisper'd me through the night, and very plainly
        before daybreak,
Lisp'd to me the low and delicious word death,
And again death, death, death, death,
Hissing melodious, neither like the bird nor like my
        arous'd child's heart,
But edging near as privately for me rustling at my feet,
Creeping thence steadily up to my ears and laving
        me softly all over,
Death, death, death, death, death.

Which I do not forget,
But fuse the song of my dusky demon and brother,
That he sang to me in the moonlight on Paumanok's
        gray beach,
With the thousand responsive songs at random,
My own songs awaked from that hour,
And with them the key, the word up from the waves,
The word of the sweetest song and all songs,
That strong and delicious word which, creeping to my feet,
(Or like some old crone rocking the cradle, swathed
        in sweet garments, bending aside,)
The sea whisper'd me.

[1859]

AS I EBB'D WITH THE OCEAN OF LIFE

1

As I ebb'd with the ocean of life,
As I wended the shores I know,
As I walk'd where the ripples continually wash you
    Paumanok,
Where they rustle up hoarse and sibilant,
Where the fierce old mother endlessly cries for her
    castaways,
I musing late in the autumn day, gazing off southward,
Held by this electric self out of the pride of which I
    utter poems,
Was seiz'd by the spirit that trails in the lines underfoot,
The rim, the sediment that stands for all the water and
    all the land of the globe.

Fascinated, my eyes reverting from the south, dropt,
    to follow those slender windrows,
Chaff, straw, splinters of wood, weeds, and the sea-gluten,
Scum, scales from shining rocks, leaves of salt-lettuce,
    left by the tide,
Miles walking, the sound of breaking waves the
    other side of me,
Paumanok there and then as I thought the old thought
    of likenesses,
These you presented to me you fish-shaped island,
As I wended the shores I know,
As I walk'd with that electric self seeking types.

2

As I wend to the shores I know not,
As I list to the dirge, the voices of men and women wreck'd,

As I inhale the impalpable breezes that set in upon me,
As the ocean so mysterious rolls toward me closer and closer,
I too but signify at the utmost a little wash'd-up drift,
A few sands and dead leaves to gather,
Gather, and merge myself as part of the sands and drift.

O baffled, balk'd, bent to the very earth,
Oppress'd with myself that I have dared to open my mouth,
Aware now that amid all that blab whose echoes recoil upon
        me I have not once had the least idea who or what I am,
But that before all my arrogant poems the real Me stands
        yet untouch'd, untold, altogether unreach'd,
Withdrawn far, mocking me with mock-congratulatory
        signs and bows,
With peals of distant ironical laughter at every word
        I have written,
Pointing in silence to these songs, and then to the
        sand beneath.

I perceive I have not really understood any thing not a
        single object, and that no man ever can,
Nature here in sight of the sea taking advantage of me
        to dart upon me and sting me,
Because I have dared to open my mouth to sing at all.

        3
You oceans both, I close with you,
We murmur alike reproachfully rolling sands and drift,
        knowing not why,
These little shreds indeed standing for you and me
        and all.

You friable shore with trails of debris,
You fish-shaped island, I take what is underfoot,
What is yours is mine my father.

I too Paumanok,
I too have bubbled up, floated the measureless float,
    and been wash'd on your shores,
I too am but a trail of drift and debris,
I too leave little wrecks upon you, you fish-shaped island.

I throw myself upon your breast my father,
I cling to you so that you cannot unloose me,
I hold you so firm till you answer me something.

Kiss me my father,
Touch me with your lips as I touch those I love,
Breathe to me while I hold you close the secret of the
    murmuring I envy.

        4
Ebb, ocean of life, (the flow will return,)
Cease not your moaning you fierce old mother,
Endlessly cry for your castaways, but fear not, deny not me,
Rustle not up so hoarse and angry against my feet as
    I touch you or gather from you.

I mean tenderly by you and all,
I gather for myself and for this phantom looking down
    where we lead, and following me and mine.

Me and mine, loose windrows, little corpses,
Froth, snowy white, and bubbles,
(See, from my dead lips the ooze exuding at last,
See, the prismatic colors glistening and rolling,)
Tufts of straw, sands, fragments,
Buoy'd hither from many moods, one contradicting another,
From the storm, the long calm, the darkness, the swell,
Musing, pondering, a breath, a briny tear, a dab of
    liquid or soil,
Up just as much out of fathomless workings fermented
    and thrown.

A limp blossom or two, torn, just as much over waves
 floating, drifted at random,
Just as much for us that sobbing dirge of Nature,
Just as much whence we come that blare of the
 cloud-trumpets,
We, capricious, brought hither we know not whence,
 spread out before you,
You up there walking or sitting,
Whoever you are, we too lie in drifts at your feet.

[1860]

ME IMPERTURBE

Me imperturbe, standing at ease in Nature,
Master of all or mistress of all, aplomb in the midst of
 irrational things,
Imbued as they, passive, receptive, silent as they,
Finding my occupation, poverty, notoriety, foibles, crimes,
 less important than I thought,
Me toward the Mexican sea, or in the Mannahatta or
 the Tennessee, or far north or inland,
A river man, or a man of the woods, or of any farm-life
 of these States or of the coast, or the lakes or Kanada,
Me wherever my life is lived, O to be self-balanced for
 contingencies,
To confront night, storms, hunger, ridicule, accidents,
 rebuffs, as the trees and animals do.

[1860]

I HEAR AMERICA SINGING

I hear America singing, the varied carols I hear,
Those of mechanics, each one singing his as it should be
    blithe and strong,
The carpenter singing his as he measures his plank or beam,
The mason singing his as he makes ready for work, or
    leaves off work,
The boatman singing what belongs to him in his boat,
    the deckhand singing on the steamboat deck,
The shoemaker singing as he sits on his bench, the hatter
    singing as he stands,
The wood-cutter's song, the ploughboy's on his way in the
    morning, or at noon intermission or at sundown,
The delicious singing of the mother, or of the young wife
    at work, or of the girl sewing or washing.
Each singing what belongs to him or her and to none else,
The day what belongs to the day—at night the party of
    young fellows, robust, friendly,
Singing with open mouths their strong melodious songs.

[1860]

POETS TO COME

Poets to come! orators, singers, musicians to come!
Not to-day is to justify me and answer what I am for,
But you, a new brood, native, athletic, continental, greater
    than before known,
Arouse! for you must justify me.

I myself but write one or two indicative words for the future,
I but advance a moment only to wheel and hurry back
    in the darkness.

I am a man who, sauntering along without fully stopping,
    turns a casual look upon you and then averts his face,
Leaving it to you to prove and define it,
Expecting the main things from you.

[1860]

FROM PENT-UP ACHING RIVERS

From pent-up aching rivers,
From that of myself without which I were nothing,
From what I am determin'd to make illustrious, even
    if I stand sole among men,
From my own voice resonant, singing the phallus,
Singing the song of procreation,
Singing the need of superb children and therein superb
    grown people,
Singing the muscular urge and the blending,
Singing the bedfellow's song. (O resistless yearning!
O for any and each the body correlative attracting!
O for you whoever you are your correlative body! O it,
    more than all else, you delighting!)
From the hungry gnaw that eats me night and day,
From native moments, from bashful pains, singing them,
Seeking something yet unfound though I have diligently
    sought it many a long year,
Singing the true song of the soul fitful at random,
Renascent with grossest Nature or among animals,
Of that, of them and what goes with them my poems
    informing.
Of the smell of apples and lemons, of the pairing of birds,
Of the wet of woods, of the lapping of waves,
Of the mad pushes of waves upon the land, I them chanting,
The overture lightly sounding, the strain anticipating,
The welcome nearness, the sight of the perfect body,
The swimmer swimming naked in the bath, or motionless
    on his back lying and floating,
The female form approaching, I pensive, love-flesh
    tremulous aching.
The divine list for myself or you or for any one making.

The face, the limbs, the index from head to foot, and
      what it arouses,
The mystic deliria, the madness amorous, the utter
      abandonment,
(Hark close and still what I now whisper to you,
I love you, O you entirely possess me,
O that you and I escape from the rest and go utterly off,
      free and lawless,
Two hawks in the air, two fishes swimming in the sea not
      more lawless than we;)
The furious storm through me careering, I passionately
      trembling,
The oath of the inseparableness of two together, of the
      woman that loves me and whom I love more
      than my life, that oath swearing.
(O I willingly stake all for you,
O let me be lost if it must be so!
O you and I! what is it to us what the rest do or think?
What is all else to us? only that we enjoy each other and
      exhaust each other if it must be so;)
From the master, the pilot I yield the vessel to,
The general commanding me, commanding all, from
      him permission taking,
From time the programme hastening, (I have loiter'd
      too long as it is,)
From sex, from the warp and from the woof,
From privacy, from frequent repinings alone,
From plenty of persons near and yet the right person
      not near,
From the soft sliding of hands over me and thrusting of
      fingers through my hair and beard,
From the long sustain'd kiss upon the mouth or bosom,
From the close pressure that makes me or any man
      drunk, fainting with excess,
From what the divine husband knows, from the work of
      fatherhood,

From exultation, victory and relief, from the bedfellow's
    embrace in the night,
From the act-poems of eyes, hands, hips and bosoms,
From the cling of the trembling arm,
From the bending curve and the clinch,
From side by side the pliant coverlet off-throwing,
From the one so unwilling to have me leave, and me
    just as unwilling to leave,
(Yet a moment O tender waiter, and I return,)
From the hour of shining stars and dropping dews,
From the night a moment I emerging flitting out,
Celebrate you act divine and you children prepared for,
And you stalwart loins.

                                 [1860]

ONCE I PASS'D THROUGH
A POPULOUS CITY

Once I pass'd through a populous city imprinting my brain
    for future use with its shows, architecture, customs,
    traditions,
Yet now of all that city I remember only a woman I casually
    met there who detain'd me for love of me,
Day by day and night by night we were together—all else has
    long been forgotten by me,
I remember I say only that woman who passionately clung
    to me,
Again we wander, we love, we separate again,
Again she holds me by the hand, I must not go,
I see her close beside me with silent lips sad and tremulous.

                                   [1860]

NATIVE MOMENTS

Native moments—when you come upon me—ah you are
    here now,
Give me now libidinous joys only,
Give me the drench of my passions, give me life coarse
    and rank,
To-day I go consort with Nature's darlings, to-night too,
I am for those who believe in loose delights, I share
    the midnight orgies of young men,
I dance with the dancers and drink with the drinkers,
The echoes ring with our indecent calls, I pick out some low
    person for my dearest friend,
He shall be lawless, rude, illiterate, he shall be one condemn'd
    by others for deeds done,
I will play a part no longer, why should I exile myself
    from my companions?
O you shunn'd persons, I at least do not shun you,
I come forthwith in your midst, I will be your poet,
I will be more to you than to any of the rest.

                             [1860]

FACING WEST FROM CALIFORNIA'S SHORES

Facing west from California's shores,
Inquiring, tireless, seeking what is yet unfound,
I, a child, very old, over waves, towards the house of maternity,
    the land of migrations, look afar,
Look off the shores of my Western sea, the circle almost circled;
For starting westward from Hindustan, from the vales of
    Kashmere,
From Asia, from the north, from the God, the sage, and the
    hero,
From the south, from the flowery peninsulas and the spice
    islands,
Long having wander'd since, round the earth having wander'd,
Now I face home again, very pleas'd and joyous,
(But where is what I started for so long ago?
And why is it yet unfound?)

                        [1860]

AS ADAM EARLY IN THE MORNING

As Adam early in the morning,
Walking forth from the bower refresh'd with sleep,
Behold me where I pass, hear my voice, approach,
Touch me, touch the palm of your hand to my body as I pass,
Be not afraid of my body.

                        [1861]

SCENTED HERBAGE OF MY BREAST

Scented herbage of my breast,
Leaves from you I glean, I write, to be perused best afterwards,
Tomb-leaves, body-leaves growing up above me above death,
Perennial roots, tall leaves, O the winter shall not freeze
    you delicate leaves,
Every year shall you bloom again, out from where you
    retired you shall emerge again;
O I do not know whether many passing by will discover
    you or inhale your faint odor, but I believe a few will;
O slender leaves! O blossoms of my blood! I permit you
    to tell in your own way of the heart that is under you,
O I do not know what you mean there underneath
    yourselves, you are not happiness,
You are often more bitter than I can bear, you burn
    and sting me,
Yet you are beautiful to me you faint tinged roots,
    you make me think of death,
Death is beautiful from you, (what indeed is finally
    beautiful except death and love?)
O I think it is not for life I am chanting here my chant
    of lovers, I think it must be for death,
For how calm, how solemn it grows to ascend to the
    atmosphere of lovers,
Death or life I am then indifferent, my soul declines
    to prefer,
I am not sure but the high soul of lovers welcomes
    death most,)
Indeed O death, I think now these leaves mean precisely
    the same as you mean,
Grow up taller sweet leaves that I may see! grow up out of
    my breast!
Spring away from the conceal'd heart there!

Do not fold yourself so in your pink-tinged roots timid
  leaves!
Do not remain down there so ashamed, herbage of my breast!
Come I am detemin'd to unbare this broad breast of
  mine, I have long enough stifled and choked;
Emblematic and capricious blades I leave you,
    now you serve me not,
I will say what I have to say by itself,
I will sound myself and comrades only, I will never
    again utter a call only their call,
I will raise with it immortal reverberations through the States,
I will give an example to lovers to take permanent shape and
  will through the States,
Through me shall the words be said to make death
  exhilarating,
Give me your tone therefore O death, that I may accord
  with it,
Give me yourself, for I see that you belong to me now
    above all, and are folded inseparably together, you
    love and death are,
Nor will I allow you to balk me any more with what
  I was calling life,
For now it is convey'd to me that you are the purports
  essential,
That you hide in these shifting forms of life, for reasons,
  and that they are mainly for you,
That you beyond them come forth to remain, the real
  reality,
That behind the mask of materials you patiently wait,
  no matter how long,
That you will one day perhaps take control of all,
That you will perhaps dissipate this entire show of appearance,
That may-be you are what it is all for, but it does not
  last so very long,
But you will last very long.

[1860]

BEAT! BEAT! DRUMS!

Beat! beat! drums!—blow! bugles! blow!
Through the windows—through doors—burst like a ruthless
    force,
Into the solemn church, and scatter the congregation,
Into the school where the scholar is studying;
Leave not the bridegroom quiet—no happiness must he
    have now with his bride,
Nor the peaceful farmer any peace, ploughing his field
    or gathering his grain,
So fierce you whirr and pound you drums—so shrill you
    bugles blow.

Beat! beat! drums!—blow! bugles! blow!
Over the traffic of cities—over the rumble of wheels in the
    streets;
Are beds prepared for sleepers at night in the houses?
    no sleepers must sleep in those beds,
No bargainers' bargains by day—no brokers or
    speculators—would they continue?
Would the talkers be talking? would the singer attempt
    to sing?
Would the lawyer rise in the court to state his case before the
    judge?
Then rattle quicker, heavier drums—you bugles wilder blow.

Beat! beat! drums!—blow! bugles! blow!
Make no parley—stop for no expostulation,
Mind not the timid—mind not the weeper or prayer,
Mind not the old man beseeching the young man,
Let not the child's voice be heard, nor the mother's
    entreaties,

Make even the trestles to shake the dead where they lie
    awaiting the hearses,
So strong you thump O terrible drums—so loud you
    bugles blow.

                              [1861]

CITY OF SHIPS

City of ships!
(O the black ships! O the fierce ships!
O the beautiful sharp-bow'd steam-ships and sail-ships!)
City of the world! (for all races are here,
All the lands of the earth make contributions here;)
City of the sea! city of hurried and glittering tides!
City whose gleeful tides continually rush or recede,
    whirling in and out with eddies and foam!
City of wharves and stores—city of tall façades of marble
    and iron!
Proud and passionate city—mettlesome, mad, extravagant
    city!
Spring up O city—not for peace alone, but be indeed
    yourself, warlike!
Fear not—submit to no models but your own O city!
Behold me—incarnate me as I have incarnated you!
I have rejected nothing you offer'd me—whom you adopted
    I have adopted,
Good or bad I never question you—I love all—
    I do not condemn any thing,
I chant and celebrate all that is yours—yet peace no more,
In peace I chanted peace, but now the drum of war is mine,
War, red war is my song through your streets, O city!

                              [1865]

CAVALRY CROSSING A FORD

A line in long array where they wind betwixt green islands,
They take a serpentine course, their arms flash in the sun—
    hark to the musical clank,
Behold the silvery river, in it the splashing horses loitering
    stop to drink,
Behold the brown-faced men, each group, each person
    a picture, the negligent rest on the saddles,
Some emerge on the opposite bank, others are just
    entering the ford—while,
Scarlet and blue and snowy white,
The guidon flags flutter gayly in the wind.

[1865]

BIVOUAC ON A MOUNTAIN SIDE

I see before me now a traveling army halting,
Below a fertile valley spread, with barns and the
    orchards of summer,
Behind, the terraced sides of a mountain, abrupt, in
    places rising high,
Broken, with rocks, with clinging cedars, with tall shapes
    dingily seen,
The numerous camp-fires scatter'd near and far, some
    away up on the mountain,
The shadowy forms of men and horses, looming, large-sized,
    flickering,
And over all the sky—the sky! far, far out of reach,
    studded, breaking out, the eternal stars.

[1865]

AN ARMY CORPS ON THE MARCH

With its cloud of skirmishers in advance,
With now the sound of a single shot snapping like a whip,
    and now an irregular volley,
The swarming ranks press on and on, the dense brigades
    press on,
Glittering dimly, toiling under the sun—the dust-cover'd
    men,
In columns rise and fall to the undulations of the ground,
With artillery interspers'd—the wheels rumble, the
    horses sweat,
As the army corps advances.

[1865–66]

BY THE BIVOUAC'S FITFUL FLAME

By the bivouac's fitful flame,
A procession winding around me, solemn and sweet and
    slow—but first I note,
The tents of the sleeping army, the fields' and woods'
    dim outline,
The darkness lit by spots of kindled fire, the silence,
Like a phantom far or near an occasional figure moving,
The shrubs and trees, (as I lift my eyes they seem to be
    stealthily watching me,)
While wind in procession thoughts, O tender and wondrous
    thoughts,
Of life and death, of home and the past and loved, and
    of those that are far away;
A solemn and slow procession there as I sit on the ground,
By the bivouac's fitful flame.

[1865]

COME UP FROM THE FIELDS FATHER

Come up from the fields father, here's a letter from
    our Pete,
And come to the front door mother, here's a letter from
    thy dear son.

Lo, 'tis autumn,
Lo, where the trees, deeper green, yellower and redder,
Cool and sweeten Ohio's villages with leaves fluttering in the
    moderate wind,
Where apples ripe in the orchards hang and grapes on
    the trellis'd vines,
(Smell you the smell of the grapes on the vines?
Smell you the buckwheat where the bees were lately
    buzzing?)

Above all, lo, the sky so calm, so transparent after the
    rain, and with wondrous clouds,
Below too, all calm, all vital and beautiful, and the farm
    prospers well.

Down in the fields all prospers well,
But now from the fields come father, come at the
    daughter's call,
And come to the entry mother, to the front door come
    right away.

Fast as she can she hurries, something ominous, her steps
    trembling,
She does not tarry to smooth her hair nor adjust her cap.

Open the envelope quickly,
O this is not our son's writing, yet his name is sign'd,

O a strange hand writes for our dear son, O stricken
    mother's soul!
All swims before her eyes, flashes with black, she catches
    the main words only,
Sentences broken, *gunshot wound in the breast, cavalry
    skirmish, taken to hospital,*
At present low, but will soon be better.

Ah now the single figure to me,
Amid all teeming and wealthy Ohio with all its cities and
    farms,
Sickly white in the face and dull in the head, very faint,
By the jamb of a door leans.

Grieve not so, dear mother, (the just-grown daughter
    speaks through her sobs,
The little sisters huddle around speechless and dismay'd,)
*See, dearest mother, the letter says Pete will soon be
    better.*

Alas poor boy, he will never be better, (nor may-be
    needs to be better, that brave and simple soul,)
While they stand at home at the door he is dead already,
The only son is dead.

But the mother needs to be better,
She with thin form presently drest in black,
By day her meals untouch'd then at night fitfully sleeping,
    often waking,
In the midnight waking, weeping, longing with one deep
    longing,
O that she might withdraw unnoticed, silent from life
    escape and withdraw,
To follow, to seek, to be with her dear dead son.

                         [1865]

VIGIL STRANGE I KEPT ON
THE FIELD ONE NIGHT

Vigil strange I kept on the field one night;
When you my son and my comrade dropt at my side
    that day,
One look I but gave which your dear eyes return'd with
    a look I shall never forget,
One touch of your hand to mine O boy, reach'd up as
    you lay on the ground,
Then onward I sped in the battle, the even-contested battle,
Till late in the night reliev'd to the place at last again
    I made my way,
Found you in death so cold dear comrade, found your
    body son of responding kisses, (never again
    on earth responding,)
Bared your face in the starlight, curious the scene, cool
    blew the moderate night-wind,
Long there and then in vigil I stood, dimly around me
    the battle-field spreading,
Vigil wondrous and vigil sweet there in the fragrant
    silent night,
But not a tear fell, not even a long-drawn sigh, long, long
    I gazed,
Then on the earth partially reclining sat by your side
    leaning my chin in my hands,
Passing sweet hours, immortal and mystic hours with
    you dearest comrade—not a tear, not a word,
Vigil of silence, love and death, vigil for you my son
    and my soldier,
As onward silently stars aloft, eastward new ones upward
    stole,
Vigil final for you brave boy, (I could not save you,
    swift was your death,

I faithfully loved you and cared for you living, I think
    we shall surely meet again,)
Till at latest lingering of the night, indeed just as the
    dawn appear'd,
My comrade I wrapt in his blanket, envelop'd well his form,
Folded the blanket well, tucking it carefully over head
    and carefully under feet,
And there and then and bathed by the rising sun, my son
    in his grave, in his rude-dug grave I deposited,
Ending my vigil strange with that, vigil of night and
    battle-field dim,
Vigil for boy of responding kisses, (never again on earth
    responding,)
Vigil for comrade swiftly slain, vigil I never forget,
    how as day brighten'd,
I rose from the chill ground and folded my soldier
    well in his blanket,
And buried him where he fell.

[1865]

A MARCH IN THE RANKS HARD-PREST, AND THE ROAD UNKNOWN

A march in the ranks hard-prest, and the road unknown,
A route through a heavy wood with muffled steps in
    the darkness,
Our army foil'd with loss severe, and the sullen remnant
    retreating,
Till after midnight glimmer upon us the lights of a
    dim-lighted building,
We come to an open space in the woods, and halt by
    the dim-lighted building,
'Tis a large old church at the crossing roads, now an
    impromptu hospital,
Entering but for a minute I see a sight beyond all the
    pictures and poems ever made,
Shadows of deepest, deepest black, just lit by moving candles
    and lamps,
And by one great pitchy torch stationary with wild red
    flame and clouds of smoke,
By these, crowds, groups of forms vaguely I see on the
    floor, some in the pews laid down,
At my feet more distinctly a soldier, a mere lad,
    in danger of bleeding to death, (he is shot in the
    abdomen,)
I stanch the blood temporarily, (the youngster's face is
    white as a lily,)
Then before I depart I sweep my eyes o'er the scene
    fain to absorb it all,
Faces, varieties, postures beyond description, most in
    obscurity, some of them dead,
Surgeons operating, attendants holding lights, the smell of
    ether, the odor of blood,

The crowd, O the crowd of the bloody forms, the yard
    outside also fill'd,
Some on the bare ground, some on planks or stretchers,
    some in the death-spasm sweating,
An occasional scream or cry, the doctor's shouted
    orders or calls,
The glisten of the little steel instruments catching the
    glint of the torches,
These I resume as I chant, I see again the forms, I smell
    the odor,
Then hear outside the orders given, *Fall in, my men, fall in;*
But first I bend to the dying lad, his eyes open, a half-smile
    gives he me,
Then the eyes close, calmly close, and I speed forth
    to the darkness,
Resuming, marching, ever in darkness marching,
    on in the ranks,
The unknown road still marching.

                                                    [1865]

A SIGHT IN CAMP IN THE DAYBREAK GRAY AND DIM

A sight in camp in the daybreak gray and dim,
As from my tent I emerge so early sleepless,
As slow I walk in the cool fresh air the path near by the
    hospital tent,
Three forms I see on stretchers lying, brought out there
    untended lying,
Over each the blanket spread, ample brownish woolen
    blanket,
Gray and heavy blanket, folding, covering all.

Curious I halt and silent stand,
Then with light fingers I from the face of the nearest
    the first just lift the blanket;
Who are you elderly man so gaunt and grim, with well-gray'd
    hair, and flesh all sunken about the eyes?
Who are you my dear comrade?
Then to the second I step—and who are you my child
    and darling?
Who are you sweet boy with cheeks yet blooming?

Then to the third—a face nor child nor old, very calm,
    as of beautiful yellow-white ivory;
Young man I think I know you—I think this face is
    the face of the Christ himself,
Dead and divine and brother of all, and here again he lies.
                                            [1865]

AS TOILSOME I WANDER'D
VIRGINIA'S WOODS

As toilsome I wander'd Virginia's woods,
To the music of rustling leaves kick'd by my feet, (for 'twas
    autumn,)
I mark'd at the foot of a tree the grave of a soldier;
Mortally wounded he and buried on the retreat, (easily
    all could I understand,)
The halt of a mid-day hour, when up! no time to lose—
    yet this sign left,
On a tablet scrawl'd and nail'd on the tree by the grave,
Bold, cautious, true, and my loving comrade.

Long, long I muse, then on my way go wandering,
Many a changeful season to follow, and many a scene of life,
Yet at times through changeful season and scene, abrupt,
    alone, or in the crowded street,
Comes before me the unknown soldier's grave, comes
    the inscription rude in Virginia's woods,
Bold, cautious, true, and my loving comrade.

                                 [1865]

THE WOUND-DRESSER

1

An old man bending I come among new faces,
Years looking backward resuming in answer to children,
Come tell us old man, as from young men and
      maidens that love me,
(Arous'd and angry, I'd thought to beat the alarum, and
      urge relentless war,
But soon my fingers fail'd me, my face droop'd and
      I resign'd myself,
To sit by the wounded and soothe them, or silently watch
      the dead;)
Years hence of these scenes, of these furious passions,
      these chances,
Of unsurpass'd heroes, (was one side so brave? the other
      was equally brave;)
Now be witness again, paint the mightiest armies of earth,
Of those armies so rapid so wondrous what saw
      you to tell us?
What stays with you latest and deepest? of curious panics,
Of hard-fought engagements or sieges tremendous
      what deepest remains?

2

O maidens and young men I love and that love me,
What you ask of my days those the strangest and sudden
      your talking recalls,
Soldier alert I arrive after a long march cover'd with
      sweat and dust,
In the nick of time I come, plunge in the fight, loudly
      shout in the rush of successful charge,
Enter the captur'd works—yet lo, like a swift-running river
      they fade,

Pass and are gone they fade—I dwell not on soldiers'
    perils or soldiers' joys,
(Both I remember well—many the hardships, few the
    joys, yet I was content.)

But in silence, in dreams' projections,
While the world of gain and appearance and mirth
    goes on,
So soon what is over forgotten, and waves wash the
    imprints off the sand,
With hinged knees returning I enter the doors, (while for
    you up there,
Whoever you are, follow without noise and be of
    strong heart.)

Bearing the bandages, water and sponge,
Straight and swift to my wounded I go,
Where they lie on the ground after the battle brought in,
Where their priceless blood reddens the grass the ground,
Or to the rows of the hospital tent, or under the
    roof'd hospital,
To the long rows of cots up and down each side I return,
To each and all one after another I draw near, not
    one do I miss,
An attendant follows holding a tray, he carries a refuse pail,
Soon to be fill'd with clotted rags and blood, emptied,
    and fill'd again.

I onward go, I stop,
With hinged knees and steady hand to dress wounds,
I am firm with each, the pangs are sharp yet unavoidable,
One turns to me his appealing eyes—poor boy! I never
    knew you,
Yet I think I could not refuse this moment to die for
    you, if that would save you.

3

On, on I go, (open doors of time! open hospital doors!)
The crush'd head I dress, (poor crazed hand tear not
    the bandage away,)
The neck of the cavalry-man with the bullet through
    and through I examine,
Hard the breathing rattles, quite glazed already the eye,
    yet life struggles hard,
(Come sweet death! be persuaded O beautiful death!
In mercy come quickly.)

From the stump of the arm, the amputated hand,
I undo the clotted lint, remove the slough, wash off the
    matter and blood,
Back on his pillow the soldier bends with curv'd neck
    and side-falling head,
His eyes are closed, his face is pale, he dares not look on
    the bloody stump,
And has not yet look'd on it.

I dress a wound in the side, deep, deep,
But a day or two more, for see the frame all wasted
    and sinking,
And the yellow-blue countenance see.

I dress the perforated shoulder, the foot with the
    bullet-wound,
Cleanse the one with a gnawing and putrid gangrene,
    so sickening, so offensive,
While the attendant stands behind aside me holding the
    tray and pail.

I am faithful, I do not give out,
The fractur'd thigh, the knee, the wound in the abdomen,
These and more I dress with impassive hand, (yet deep
    in my breast a fire, a burning flame.)

4

Thus in silence in dreams' projections,
Returning, resuming, I thread my way through the
    hospitals,
The hurt and wounded I pacify with soothing hand,
I sit by the restless all the dark night, some are so young,
Some suffer so much, I recall the experience sweet and sad,
(Many a soldier's loving arms about this neck have
    cross'd and rested,
Many a soldier's kiss dwells on these bearded lips.)

                          [1865]

WHEN LILACS LAST IN THE
DOORYARD BLOOM'D

1

When lilacs last in the dooryard bloom'd,
And the great star early droop'd in the western sky in the
    night,
I mourn'd, and yet shall mourn with ever-returning spring.

Ever-returning spring, trinity sure to me you bring,
Lilac blooming perennial and drooping star in the west,
And thought of him I love.

2

O powerful western fallen star!
O shades of night—O moody, tearful night!
O great star disappear'd—O the black murk that hides
    the star!
O cruel hands that holds me powerless—O helpless soul
    of me!
O harsh surrounding cloud that will not free my soul.

3

In the dooryard fronting an old farm-house near the
    white-wash'd palings,
Stands the lilac-bush tall-growing with heart-shaped leaves
    of rich green,
With many a pointed blossom rising delicate, with the
    perfume strong I love,
With every leaf a miracle—and from this bush in the
    dooryard,
With delicate-color'd blossoms and heart-shaped leaves of
    rich green,
A sprig with its flower I break.

4

In the swamp in secluded recesses,
A shy and hidden bird is warbling a song.

Solitary the thrush,
The hermit withdrawn to himself, avoiding the settlements,
Sings by himself a song.

Song of the bleeding throat,
Death's outlet song of life, (for well dear brother I know,
If thou wast not granted to sing thou would'st surely die.)

5

Over the breast of the spring, the land, amid cities,
Amid lanes and through old woods, where lately the violets
    peep'd from the ground, spotting the gray debris,
Amid the grass in the fields each side of the lanes, passing
    the endless grass,
Passing the yellow-spear'd wheat, every grain from its
    shroud in the dark-brown fields uprisen,
Passing the apple-tree blows of white and pink in the
    orchards,
Carrying a corpse to where it shall rest in the grave,
Night and day journeys a coffin.

6

Coffin that passes through lanes and streets,
Through day and night with the great cloud darkening
    the land,
With the pomp of the inloop'd flags with the cities draped
    in black,
With the show of the States themselves as of crape-veil'd
    women standing,
With processions long and winding and the flambeaus
    of the night,
With the countless torches lit, with the silent sea of faces
    and the unbared heads,
With the waiting depot, the arriving coffin, and the sombre
    faces,
With dirges through the night, with the thousand voices
    rising strong and solemn,
With all the mournful voices of the dirges pour'd around
    the coffin,
The dim-lit churches and the shuddering organs—where
    amid these you journey,
With the tolling tolling bells' perpetual clang,
Here, coffin that slowly passes,
I give you my sprig of lilac.

7

(Nor for you, for one alone,
Blossoms and branches green to coffins all I bring,
For fresh as the morning, thus would I chant a song for you
    O sane and sacred death.

All over bouquets of roses,
O death, I cover you over with roses and early lilies,
But mostly and now the lilac that blooms the first,
Copious I break, I break the sprigs from the bushes,
With loaded arms I come, pouring for you,
For you and the coffins all of you O death.)

8

O western orb sailing the heaven,
Now I know what you must have meant as a month since I
    walk'd,
As I walk'd in silence the transparent shadowy night,
As I saw you had something to tell as you bent to me night
    after night,
As you droop'd from the sky low down as if to my side,
    (while the other stars all look'd on,)
As we wander'd together the solemn night, (for something
    I know not what kept me from sleep,)
As the night advanced, and I saw on the rim of the west
    how full you were of woe,
As I stood on the rising ground in the breeze in the cool
    transparent night,
As I watch'd where you pass'd and was lost in the
    netherward black of the night,
As my soul in its trouble dissatisfied sank, as where you
    sad orb,
Concluded, dropt in the night, and was gone.

9

Sing on there in the swamp,
O singer bashful and tender, I hear your notes, I hear
    your call,
I hear, I come presently, I understand you,
But a moment I linger, for the lustrous star has detain'd me,
The star my departing comrade holds and detains me.

10

O how shall I warble myself for the dead one there I loved?
And how shall I deck my song for the large sweet soul
    that has gone?
And what shall my perfume be for the grave of him I love?

Sea-winds blown from east and west,
Blown from the Eastern sea and blown from the Western
    sea, till there on the prairies meeting,
These and with these and the breath of my chant,
I'll perfume the grave of him I love.

11

O what shall I hang on the chamber walls?
And what shall the pictures be that I hang on the walls,
To adorn the burial-house of him I love?

Pictures of growing spring and farms and homes,
With the Fourth-month eve at sundown, and the gray
    smoke lucid and bright,
With floods of the yellow gold of the gorgeous, indolent,
    sinking sun, burning, expanding the air,
With the fresh sweet herbage under foot, and the pale green
    leaves of the trees prolific,
In the distance the flowing glaze, the breast of the river,
    with a wind-dapple here and there,
With ranging hills on the banks, with many a line against
    the sky, and shadows,
And the city at hand with dwellings so dense, and stacks of
    chimneys,
And all the scene of life and the workshops, and the
    workmen homeward returning.

12

Lo, body and soul—this land,
My own Manhattan with spires, and the sparkling and
    hurrying tides, and the ships,
The varied and ample land, the South and the North in the
    light, Ohio's shores and flashing Missouri,
And ever the far-spreading prairies cover'd with grass
    and corn.

Lo, the most excellent sun so calm and haughty,
The violet and purple morn with just-felt breezes,
The gentle soft-born measureless light,
The miracle spreading bathing all, the fulfill'd noon,
The coming eve delicious, the welcome night and the stars,
Over my cities shining all, enveloping man and land.

13

Sing on, sing on you gray-brown bird,
Sing from the swamps, the recesses, pour your chant from
    the bushes,
Limitless out of the dusk, out of the cedars and pines.

Sing on dearest brother, warble your reedy song,
Loud human song, with voice of uttermost woe,

O liquid and free and tender!
O wild and loose to my soul—O wondrous singer!
You only I hear—yet the star holds me, (but will soon
    depart,)
Yet the lilac with mastering odor holds me.

14

Now while I sat in the day and look'd forth,
In the close of the day with its light and the fields of spring,
    and the farmers preparing their crops,
In the large unconscious scenery of my land with its lakes
    and forests,
In the heavenly aerial beauty, (after the perturb'd winds
    and the storms,)
Under the arching heavens of the afternoon swift passing,
    and the voices of children and women,
The many-moving sea-tides, and I saw the ships how they
    sail'd,
And the summer approaching with richness, and the fields
    all busy with labor,

And the infinite separate houses, how they all went on,
    each with its meals and minutia of daily usages,
And the streets how their throbbings throbb'd, and the
    cities pent—lo, then and there,
Falling upon them all and among them all, enveloping me
    with the rest,
Appear'd the cloud, appear'd the long black trail,
And I knew death, its thought, and the sacred knowledge
    of death.

Then with the knowledge of death as walking one side of me,
And the thought of death close-walking the other side of me,
And I in the middle as with companions, and as holding
    the hands of companions,
I fled forth to the hiding receiving night that talks not,
Down to the shores of the water, the path by the swamp
    in the dimness,
To the solemn shadowy cedars and ghostly pines so still.

And the singer so shy to the rest receiv'd me,
The gray-brown bird I know receiv'd us comrades three,
And he sang the carol of death, and a verse for him I love.

From deep secluded recesses,
From the fragrant cedars and the ghostly pines so still,
Came the carol of the bird.

And the charm of the carol rapt me,
As I held as if by their hands my comrades in the night,
And the voice of my spirit tallied the song of the bird.

Come lovely and soothing death,
Undulate round the world, serenely arriving, arriving,

In the day, in the night, to all, to each,
Sooner or later delicate death.

Prais'd be the fathomless universe,
For life and joy, and for objects and knowledge curious,
And for love, sweet love—but praise! praise! praise!
For the sure-enwinding arms of cool-enfolding death.

Dark mother always gliding near with soft feet,
Have none chanted for thee a chant of fullest welcome?
Then I chant it foe thee, I glorify thee above all,
I bring thee a song that when thou must indeed come,
    come unfalteringly.

Approach strong deliveress,
When it is so, when thou hast taken them I joyously sing
    the dead,
Lost in the loving floating ocean of thee,
Laved in the flood of thy bliss O death.

From me to thee glad serenades,
Dances for thee I propose saluting thee, adornments and
    feastings for thee,
And the sights of the open landscape and the high-spread
    sky are fitting,
And life and the fields, and the huge and thoughtful night.

The night in silence under many a star,
The ocean shore and the husky whispering wave whose
    voice I know,
And the soul turning to thee O vast and well-veil'd death,
And the body gratefully nestling close to thee.

Over the tree-tops I float thee a song,
Over the rising and sinking waves, over the myriad fields
    and the prairies wide,
Over the dense-pack'd cities all and the teeming wharves
    and ways,
I float this carol with joy, with joy to thee O death.

15

To the tally of my soul,
Loud and strong kept up the gray-brown bird,
With pure deliberate notes spreading filling the night.

Loud in the pines and cedars dim,
Clear in the freshness moist and the swamp-perfume,
And I with my comrades there in the night.

While my sight that was bound in my eyes unclosed,
As to long panoramas of visions.

And I saw askant the armies,
I saw as in noiseless dreams hundreds of battle-flags,
Borne through the smoke of the battles and pierc'd with
        missiles I saw them,
And carried hither and you through the smoke, and torn
        and bloody,
And at last but a few shreds left on the staffs, (and all in
        silence,)
And the staffs all splinter'd and broken.

I saw battle-corpses, myriads of them,
And the white skeletons of young men, I saw them,
I saw the debris and debris of all the slain soldiers of the war,
But I saw they were not as was thought,
They themselves were fully at rest, they suffer'd not,
The living remain'd and suffer'd, the mother suffer'd,
And the wife and the child and the musing comrade suffer'd,
And the armies that remain'd suffer'd.

16

Passing the visions, passing the night,
Passing, unloosing the hold of my comrades' hands,
Passing the song of the hermit bird and the tallying song
    of my soul,
Victorious song, death's outlet song, yet varying
    ever-altering song.

As low and wailing, yet clear the notes, rising and falling,
    flooding the night,
Sadly sinking and fainting, as warning and warning, and
    yet again bursting with joy,
Covering the earth and filling the spread of the heaven,
As that powerful psalm in the night I heard from recesses,
Passing, I leave thee lilac with heart-shaped leaves,
I leave thee there in the door-yard, blooming, returning
    with spring.

I cease from my song for thee,
From my gaze on thee in the west, fronting the west,
    communing with thee,
O comrade lustrous with silver face in the night.

Yet each to keep and all, retrievements out of the night,
The song, the wondrous chant of the gray-brown bird,
And the tallying chant, the echo arous'd in my soul,
With the lustrous and drooping star with the countenance
    full of woe,
With the holders holding my hand nearing the call of
    the bird,
Comrades mine and I in the midst, and their memory ever
    to keep, for the dead I loved so well,
For the sweetest, wisest soul of all my days and lands—and
    this for his dear sake,
Lilac and star and bird twined with the chant of my soul,
There in the fragrant pines and the cedars dusk and dim.

                         [1865–66]

O CAPTAIN! MY CAPTAIN!

O Captain! my Captain! our fearful trip is done,
The ship has weather'd every rack, the prize we sought
    is won,
The port is near, the bells I hear, the people all exulting.
While follow eyes the steady keel, the vessel grim and daring;
        But O heart! heart! heart!
       O the bleeding drops of red,
          Where on the deck my Captain lies,
          Fallen cold and dead.

O Captain! my Captain! rise up and hear the bells;
Rise up—for you the flag is flung—for you the bugle trills,
For you bouquets and ribbon'd wreaths—for you the
    shores a-crowding,
For you they call, the swaying mass, their eager faces turning;
        Here Captain! dear father!
       This arm beneath your head!
          It is some dream that on the deck,
          You've fallen cold and dead.

My Captain does not answer, his lips are pale and still,
My father does not feel my arm, he has no pulse nor will,
The ship is anchor'd safe and sound, its voyage closed
    and done,
From fearful trip the victor ship comes in with object won;
        Exult O shores, and ring O bells!
       But I with mournful tread,
          Walk the deck my Captain lies,
          Fallen cold and dead.

                    [1865–66]

ONE'S-SELF I SING

One's-Self I sing, a simple separate person,
Yet utter the word Democratic, the word En-Masse.

Of physiology from top to toe I sing,
Not physiognomy alone nor brain alone is worthy for
    the Muse, I say the Form complete is worthier far,
The Female equally with the Male I sing.

Of Life immense in passion, pulse, and power,
Cheerful, for freest action form'd under the laws divine,
The Modern Man I sing.

[1867]

A NOISELESS PATIENT SPIDER

A noiseless patient spider,
I mark'd where on a little promontory it stood isolated,
Mark'd how to explore the vacant vast surrounding,
It launch'd forth filament, filament, filament, out of itself,
Ever unreeling them, ever tirelessly speeding them.

And you O my soul where you stand,
Surrounded, detached, in measureless oceans of space,
Ceaselessly musing, venturing, throwing, seeking the
    spheres to connect them,
Till the bridge you will need be form'd, till the ductile
    anchor hold,
Till the gossamer thread you fling catch somewhere,
    O my soul.

[1868]

PASSAGE TO INDIA

1

Singing my days,
Singing the great achievements of the present,
Singing the strong light works of engineers,
Our modern wonders, (the antique ponderous Seven
    outvied,)
In the Old World the east the Suez canal,
The New by its mighty railroad spann'd,
The seas inlaid with eloquent gentle wires;
Yet first to sound, and ever sound, the cry with thee O soul,
The Past! the Past! the Past!

The Past—the dark unfathom'd retrospect!
The teeming gulf—the sleepers and the shadows!
The past—the infinite greatness of the past!
For what is the present after all but a growth out of the past?
(As a projectile form'd, impell'd, passing a certain line, still
    keeps on,
So the present, utterly form'd, impell'd by the past.)

2

Passage O soul to India!
Eclaircise the myths Asiatic, the primitive fables.

Not you alone proud truths of the world,
Nor you alone ye facts of modern science,
But myths and fables of eld, Asia's, Africa's fables,
The far-darting beams of the spirit, the unloos'd dreams,
The deep diving bibles and legends,
The daring plots of the poets, the elder religions;
O you temples fairer than lilies pour'd over by the rising sun!

O you fables spurning the known, eluding the hold of the
    known, mounting to heaven!
You lofty and dazzling towers, pinnacled, red as roses,
    burnish'd with gold!
Towers of fables immortal fashion'd from mortal dreams!
You too I welcome and fully the same as the rest!
You too with joy I sing.

Passage to India!
Lo, soul, seest thou not God's purpose from the first?
The earth to be spann'd, connected by network,
The races, neighbors, to marry and be given in marriage,
The oceans to be cross'd the distant brought near,
The lands to be welded together.

A worship new I sing,
You captains, voyagers, explorers, yours,
You engineers, you architects, machinists, yours,
You, not for trade or transportation only,
But in God's name, and for thy sake O soul.

3

Passage to India!
Lo soul for thee of tableaus twain,
I see in one the Suez canal initiated, open'd,
I see the procession of steamships, the Empress Eugenie's
    leading the van,
I mark from on deck the strange landscape, the pure sky,
    the level sand in the distance,
I pass swiftly the picturesque groups, the workmen gather'd,
The gigantic dredging machines.

In one again, different, (yet thine, all thine, O soul, the
    same,)
I see over my own continent the Pacific railroad surmounting
    every barrier,

I see continual trains of cars winding along the Platte
    carrying freight and passengers,
I hear the locomotives rushing and roaring, and the shrill
    steam-whistle,
I hear the echoes reverberate through the grandest scenery
    in the world,
I cross the Laramie plains, I note the rocks in grotesque
    shapes, the buttes,
I see the plentiful larkspur and wild onions, the barren,
    colorless, sage-deserts,
I see in glimpses afar or towering immediately above me the
    great mountains, I see the Wind river and the
    Wahsatch mountains,
I see the Monument mountain and the Eagle's Nest, I pass
    the Promontory, I ascend the Nevadas,
I scan the noble Elk mountain and wind around its base,
I see the Humboldt range, I thread the valley and cross the
    river,
I see the clear waters of lake Tahoe, I see forests of majestic
    pines,
Or crossing the great desert, the alkaline plains, I behold
    enchanting mirages of waters and meadows,
Marking through these and after all, in duplicate slender
    lines,
Bridging the three or four thousand miles of land travel,
Tying the Eastern to the Western sea,
The road between Europe and Asia.

(Ah Genoese thy dream! thy dream!
Centuries after thou art laid in thy grave,
The shore thou foundest verifies thy dream.)

    4
Passage to India!
Struggles of many a captain, tales of many a sailor dead,
Over my mood stealing and spreading they come,

Like clouds and cloudlets in the unreach'd sky.
Along all history, down the slopes,
As a rivulet running, sinking now, and now again to the
surface rising,
A ceaseless thought, a varied train—lo, soul, to thee, thy
sight, they rise,
The plans, the voyages again, the expeditions;
Again Vasco de Gama sails forth,
Again the knowledge gain'd, the mariner's compass,
Lands found and nations born, thou born America,
For purpose vast, man's long probation fill'd,
Thou rondure of the world at last accomplish'd.

5

O vast Rondure, swimming in space,
Cover'd all over with visible power and beauty,
Alternate light and day and the teeming spiritual darkness,
Unspeakable high processions of sun and moon and
countless stars above,
Below, the manifold grass and waters, animals, mountains,
trees,
With inscrutable purpose, some hidden prophetic intention,
Now first it seems my thought begins to span thee.

Down from the gardens of Asia descending radiating,
Adam and Eve appear, then their myriad progeny after
them,
Wandering, yearning, curious, with restless explorations,
With questionings, baffled, formless, feverish, with
never-happy hearts,
With that sad incessant refrain, *Wherefore unsatisfied soul?*
and *Whither O mocking life?*

Ah who shall soothe these feverish children?
Who justify these restless explorations?

Who speak the secret of impassive earth?
Who bind it to us? what is this separate Nature so unnatural?
What is this earth to our affections? (unloving earth,
    without a throb to answer ours,
Cold earth, the place of graves.)

Yet soul be sure the first intent remains, and shall be
    carried out,
Perhaps even now the time has arrived.

After the seas are all cross'd (as they seem already cross'd,)
After the great captains and engineers have accomplish'd
    their work,

After the noble inventors, after the scientists, the chemist,
    the geologist, ethnologist,
Finally shall come the poet worthy that name,
The true son of God shall come singing his songs.

Then not your deeds only O voyagers, O scientists and
    inventors, shall be justified,
All these hearts as of fretted children shall be sooth'd,
All affection shall be fully responded to, the secret shall be
    told,
All these separations and gaps shall be taken up and hook'd
    and link'd together,
The whole earth, this cold, impassive, voiceless earth, shall
    be completely justified,
Trinitas divine shall be gloriously accomplish'd and
    compacted by the true son of God, the poet,
(He shall indeed pass the straits and conquer the mountains,
He shall double the cape of Good Hope to some purpose,)
Nature and Man shall be disjoin'd and diffused no more,
The true son of God shall absolutely fuse them.

6

Year at whose wide-flung door I sing!
Year of the purpose accomplish'd!
Year of the marriage of continents, climates and oceans!
(No mere doge of Venice now wedding the Adriatic,)
I see O year in you the vast terraqueous globe given and
    giving all,
Europe to Asia, Africa join'd, and they to the New World,
The lands, geographies, dancing before you, holding a
    festival garland,
As brides and bridegrooms hand in hand.

Passage to India!
Cooling airs from Caucasus far, soothing cradle of man,
The river Euphrates flowing, the past lit up again.

Lo soul, the retrospect brought forward,
The old, most populous, wealthiest of earth's lands,
The streams of the Indus and the Ganges and their many
    affluents,
(I my shores of America walking to-day behold, resuming
    all,)
The tale of Alexander on his warlike marches suddenly
    dying,
On one side China and on the other side Persia and Arabia,
To the south the great seas and the bay of Bengal,
The flowing literatures, tremendous epics, religions, castes,
Old occult Brahma interminably far back, the tender and
    junior Buddha,
Central and southern empires and all their belongings,
    possessors,
The wars of Tamerlane, the reign of Aurungzebe,
The traders, rulers, explorers, Moslems, Venetians,
    Byzantium, the Arabs, Portuguese,
The first travelers famous yet, Marco Polo, Batouta the
    Moor,
Doubts to be solv'd, the map incognita, blanks to be fill'd,

The foot of man unstay'd, the hands never at rest,
Thyself O soul that will not brook a challenge.
The mediæval navigators rise before me,
The world of 1492, with its awaken'd enterprise,
Something swelling in humanity now like the sap of the
    earth in spring,
The sunset splendor of chivalry declining.

And who art thou sad shade?
Gigantic, visionary, thyself a visionary,
With majestic limbs and pious beaming eyes,
Spreading around with every look of thine a golden world,
Enhuing it with gorgeous hues.

As the chief histrion,
Down to the footlights walks in some great scena,
Dominating the rest I see the Admiral himself,
(History's type of courage, action, faith,)
Behold him sail from Palos leading his little fleet,
His voyage behold, his return, his great fame,
His misfortunes, calumniators, behold him a prisoner,
    chain'd,
Behold his dejection, poverty, death.

(Curious in time I stand, noting the efforts of heroes,
Is the deferment long? bitter the slander, poverty, death?
Lies the seed unreck'd for centuries in the ground? lo, to
    God's due occasion,
Uprising in the night, it sprouts, blooms,
And fills the earth with use and beauty.)

7
Passage indeed OI soul to primal thought,
Not lands and seas alone, thy own clear freshness,
The young maturity of brood and bloom,
To realms of budding bibles.

O soul, repressless, I with thee and thou with me,
Thy circumnavigation of the world begin,
Of man, the voyage of his mind's return,
To reason's early paradise,
Back, back to wisdom's birth, to innocent intuitions,
Again with fair creation.

8

O we can wait no longer,
We too take ship O soul,
Joyous we too launch out on trackless seas,
Fearless for unknown shores on waves of ecstasy to sail,
Amid the wafting winds, (thou pressing me to thee, I thee
    to me, O soul,)
Caroling free, singing our song of God,
Chanting our chant of pleasant exploration.

With laugh and many a kiss,
(Let others deprecate, let others weep for sin, remorse,
    humiliation,)
O soul thou pleasest me, I thee.

Ah more than any priest O soul we too believe in God,
But with the mystery of God we dare not dally.

O soul thou pleasest me, I thee,
Sailing these seas or on the hills, or waking in the night,
Thoughts, silent thoughts, of Time and Space and Death,
    like waters flowing,
Bear me indeed as through the regions infinite,
Whose air I breathe, whose ripples hear, lave me all over,
Bathe me O God in thee, mounting to thee,
I and my soul to range in range of thee.

O Thou transcendent,
Nameless, the fibre and the breath,
Light of the light, shedding forth universes, thou centre of
    them,

Thou mightier centre of the true, the good, the loving,
Thou moral, spiritual fountain—affection's source—thou
    reservoir,
(O pensive soul of me—O thirst unsatisfied—waitest not
    there?
Waitest not haply for us somewhere there the Comrade
    perfect?)
Thou pulse—thou motive of the stars, suns, systems,
That, circling, move in order, safe, harmonious,
Athwart the shapeless vastnesses of space,
How should I think, how breathe a single breath, how
    speak, if, out of myself,
I could not launch, to those, superior universes?

Swiftly I shrivel at the thought of God,
At Nature and its wonders, Time and Space and Death,
But that I, turning, call to thee O soul, thou actual Me,
And lo, thou gently masterest the orbs,
Thou matest Time, smilest content at Death,
And fillest, swellest full the vastnesses of Space.

Greater than stars or suns,
Bounding O soul thou journeyest forth;
What love than thine and ours could wider amplify?
What aspirations, wishes, outvie thine and ours O soul?
What dreams of the ideal? what plans of purity, perfection,
    strength?
What cheerful willingness for others' sake to give up all?
For others' sake to suffer all?

Reckoning ahead O soul, when thou, the time achiev'd,
The seas all cross'd, weather'd the capes, the voyage done,
Surrounded, copest, frontest God, yieldest, the aim attain'd,
As fill'd with friendship, love complete, the Elder Brother
    found,
The Younger melts in fondness in his arms.

9

Passage to more than India!
Are thy wings plumed indeed for such far flights?
O soul, voyagest thou indeed on voyages like those?
Disportest thou on waters such as those?
Soundest below the Sanscrit and the Vedas?
Then have thy bent unleash'd.

Passage to you, your shores, ye aged fierce enigmas!
Passage to you, to mastership of you, ye strangling problems!
You, strew'd with the wrecks of skeletons, that, living,
	never reach'd you.

Passage to more than India!
O secret of the earth and sky!
Of you O waters of the sea! O winding creeks and rivers!
Of you O woods and fields! of you strong mountains of
	my land!
Of you O prairies! of you gray rocks!
O morning red! O clouds! O rain and snows!
O day and night, passage to you!

O sun and moon and all you stars! Sirius and Jupiter!
Passage to you!

Passage, immediate passage! the blood burns in my veins!
Away O soul! hoist instantly the anchor!
Cut the hawsers—haul out—shake out every sail!
Have we not stood here like trees in the ground long enough?
Have we not grovel'd here long enough, eating and drinking
	like mere brutes?
Have we not darken'd and dazed ourselves with books
	long enough?

Sail forth—steer for the deep waters only,
Reckless O soul, exploring, I with thee, and thou with me,

For we are bound where mariner has not yet dared to go,
And we will risk the ship, ourselves and all.
O my brave soul!
O farther farther sail!
O daring joy, but safe! are they not all the seas of God?
O farther, farther, farther sail!

[1871]

THE DALLIANCE OF THE EAGLES

Skirting the river road, (my forenoon walk, my rest,)
Skyward in air a sudden muffled sound, the dalliance of
    the eagles,
The rushing amorous contact high in space together,
The clinching interlocking claws, a living, fierce,
    gyrating wheel,
Four beating wings, two beaks, a swirling mass tight
    grappling,
In tumbling turning clustering loops, straight downward
    falling,
Till o'er the river pois'd, the twain yet one, a moment's lull,
A motionless still balance in the air, then parting, talons
    loosing,
Upward again on slow-firm pinions slanting, their separate
    diverse flight,
She hers, he his, pursuing.

[1880]

GOOD-BYE MY FANCY!

Good-bye my Fancy!
Farewell dear mate, dear love!
I'm going away, I know not where,
Or to what fortune, or whether I may ever see you again,
So Good-bye my Fancy.

Now for my last—let me look back a moment;
The slower fainter ticking of the clock is in me,
Exit, nightfall, and soon the heart-thud stopping.

Long have we lived, joy'd, caress'd together;
Delightful!—now separation—Good-bye my Fancy.

Yet let me not be too hasty,
Long indeed have we lived, slept, filter'd, become really
    blended into one;
Then if we die we die together, (yes, we'll remain one,)
If we go anywhere we'll go together to meet what happens,
May-be we'll be better off and blither, and learn something,
May-be it is yourself now really ushering me to the
    true songs, (who knows?)
May-be it is you the mortal knob really undoing, turning—
    so now finally,
Good-bye—and hail! my Fancy.

[1891]